Journeys Into Luke

16 Lessons of Exploration and Discovery

Raymond Apicella

Nihil Obstat: Rev. Hilarion Kistner, O.F.M.
Rev. Robert L. Hagedorn

Imprimi Potest: Rev. John Bok, O.F.M.
Provincial

Imprimatur: +James H. Garland, V.G.
Archdiocese of Cincinnati
July 25, 1991

The *nihil obstat* and *imprimatur* are a declaration that a book is considered to be free from doctrinal or moral error. It is not implied that those who have granted the *nihil obstat* and *imprimatur* agree with the contents, opinions or statements expressed.

Cover and book design by Julie Lonneman

ISBN 0-86716-144-2

Published by St. Anthony Messenger Press
Printed in the U.S.A.

Acknowledgments

No text is the work of one person alone. A number of people were key to my completing this project and deserve recognition. I am grateful to Lisa Biedenbach, managing editor of St. Anthony Messenger Press, for inviting me to write this manual as a companion to my other work, *Journeys Into Mark*. Thanks are also due to the team of the Institute for Pastoral Ministries, St. Thomas University, for their encouragement and support throughout this project. I am especially thankful to my sister, Ann Riccio, and her employer, Walter Wagoner, for assisting me in the purchase of another computer after mine died. Special thanks are due to Sister Jean Burbo, I.H.M., who, while associated with the Texas Catholic Conference, acquired a set of LaVerdiere's tapes for me and started me on my journey to understanding Luke. Deserving of my deepest gratitude is my wife, Elizabeth, who not only supported me along the way but patiently and gently critiqued my work.

Dedication

In memory of my mother—Rosalie Beirne Apicella (1903-1978).

Contents

Introduction

Journeys Into Luke is biblical material designed for the adult learner. It derives from my teaching scriptural courses to undergraduate and graduate students at St. Thomas University, as well as adults from parishes of the Archdiocese of Miami. Through these teaching experiences, I am convinced that both theoretical material and its application to the life of the community are essential to understanding the Scriptures. Therefore, the presentation of these Journeys is not offered as factual material unrelated to personal life, but as a help to the reader in his or her relationship with God. The manual's two major components, background information and reflective exercises, are equally important.

Journeys Into Luke is similar to a companion work, *Journeys Into Mark*. It is a logical sequence to my work on Mark, since many scholars attest to the fact that Luke had a copy of Mark's Gospel when writing. Moreover, Luke's Gospel is relevant to our time. Its emphasis on evangelization and the marvelous themes of joy, forgiveness, table ministry, prayer and the Spirit, women and justice make it a popular account for many of us. My own appreciation for Luke has been enhanced by the work of Reverend Eugene LaVerdiere. His in-depth study of Luke's Gospel, which he has presented in numerous books and tapes, is the foundation for many of these Journeys.

Journeys Into Luke is presented in manual form. It invites you to write in the book your impressions, ideas or insights as the start of the learning experience. The diverse responses become the basis for work within a particular Journey. Each Journey offers background information (Exploring), reflective exercises (Discovering), points for review (Looking Back) and a list of resource materials for further study (Exploring Further).

The self-paced design of the manual invites you to spend as much time as needed with any one Journey. Only one exercise, Journey 1, contains a reading section that should be completed in one sitting. Each Journey is adaptable for individual or small-group study. When used as the basis for group study, the exercises encourage communal sharing and discussion of the material.

Before You Journey

Luke writes a two-volume series as the author of the Gospel and the Book of Acts. Approximately 27 percent of the New Testament writing is attributed to Luke as author of these two volumes. Most scholars date Luke's writing at around A.D. 85 to a Gentile community from the Antioch region. Antioch, the political and cultural center of Syria, was noted as a major center for early Christians.

The dating of Luke's Gospel is based on the theory that Mark was the first Gospel writer and Luke had a copy of Mark's work. Mark wrote around A.D. 70, which is also the time of the fall of Jerusalem. Careful reading of Mark 13 suggests a historical description of the time period when the great Temple of Jerusalem was being destroyed. A reading of Luke 21:20-24, however, suggests that Jerusalem has already fallen and the Temple is already destroyed. If Luke waited to write after the destruction of Jerusalem and after receiving a copy of Mark's work, then he wrote somewhere between A.D. 80 and 90 or, as scholars have compromised, at A.D. 85.

Placing Luke's writing in the Antioch region is supported by the Book of Acts and its mention of Paul's travels. Paul, the greatest missionary of the early Church, is responsible for numerous Gentiles entering Christianity. His work of evangelization places him in a time when the Jerusalem Christian community was declining because of persecution and the Roman Christian community had not yet fully developed. This in-between time and place is centered around Antioch. Some scholars believe Luke, himself a possible convert of Paul, is writing to one of these communities converted by Paul.

Studies of Luke's writing reveal the following three points: (1) Luke 1:1-4 clearly states Luke is not an eyewitness to Jesus (Luke is commenting on the gospel passed on to him by eyewitnesses rather than offering it as his own original thought); (2) his intention is to allow the story to speak for itself; and (3) in contrast to the other Gospel writers whose works can be divided, Luke offers various themes that permeate his entire Gospel. When reading Luke, we are introduced to his themes of joy, forgiveness, the role of prayer and the Spirit, the respect for women and the place of meal and justice. These themes, rising out of evangelization activities, speak to the Gentile community of Luke's time and to Christian communities of all time.

Just as commitment to evangelization in our time has produced many martyrs in the Churches of Central and South America, Luke's missionary community is also facing suffering and persecution from the Romans. His Gospel becomes an encouragement to remain steadfast in facing these persecutions. Even more serious for Luke, however, are the internal problems of the community. In an effort to reduce the persecutions, the community is waivering from its commitment to Christianity. Again, his Gospel becomes a source of encouragement to remain steadfast despite the suffering.

We know little about the man Luke. We surmise Luke to be an intelligent man because of his superb writing style and use of the Greek language. Tradition has referred to Luke as a physician because of Paul's writing in Colossians 4:14. Paul also mentions a companion, Luke, in II Timothy 4:11 and Philemon. However, neither Paul nor the writer of Acts and the Gospel claims that all of these references are to the author of the Gospel. Historically, since the second century, we have resources that attribute this Gospel to a faithful servant by the name of Luke.

Journey 1
The Importance of Story

Elie Wiesel, the Nobel Prize winner, is credited with saying "God made man [sic] because he loves stories." Everyone loves a story. In all my years of teaching I am amazed at the difference in my students' attitudes whenever I share a story. I can see an interest in their eyes, a listening attitude and a facial expression that hints of mental gymnastics while trying to apply my story to an event from their own lives.

Stories serve numerous purposes from entertainment to profound learning. They cross cultural and generational lines while revealing insight into all of humanity. They are captivating, informative and educational.

The most fascinating stories are those that reveal to the listener an event that has a profound impact on one's life. These stories, which I refer to as "aha" experience stories, provide a glimpse into the mystery of life. They give a sense of awe and wonder as to one's place in the world and the relationship with all creation and God. Often "aha" stories are self-revelatory since they point to future lessons to be learned and become the foundation for other "aha" experiences.

Discovering

Sister Mary Chupein introduced me to the "aha" experience stories from her work on mentoring. Her instructions for relating the "aha" experience story are simple:

- Reflect on a learning experience from your life.
- Tell the experience in story form.
- On completion of the story, suggest one sign or symbol that captures the story's meaning.

Possible themes for "aha" stories could be disappointment in real life, betrayal by friends, loyalty of friends or a deeper awareness into oneself.

Discovering

The following is an "aha" story from my experience. After reading my story, you are encouraged to write your "aha" experience story.

During one Lent, I was invited to give a day of recollection to a group of physically blind people from the Archdiocese of Miami. The day's theme centered on two stories about blindness from Mark's Gospel (Mark 8:22-26; 10:46-52). Although I was uncomfortable talking about blindness with blind people, I agreed to participate in the day.

As the day grew closer, I was more anxious preparing for this day than for previous retreat days. My anxiety centered on numerous fears: fear of being with "different" people; fear of uttering an inappropriate expression like, "do you see?"; and fear of not being able to relate the biblical passages to the people's lives.

These fears stayed with me until the morning of the presentation. After meeting the group, however, my fears subsided, and by lunchtime, I was totally relaxed. During the lunch break, one retreatant sat with me and began to tell me his story of blindness.

Albert was born with retinitis pigmentosa and realized he would some day lose his sight. He was living in the Bahamas with his wife and children and was doing quite well with his job when one evening, at dinnertime, Albert's disease struck quickly. He immediately became blind. He cried out in a frenzy over the loss of his sight. While in his own state of despair, Albert could hear the evening television report of famine in Africa. With the television as background noise, Albert remembers saying to himself through his tears, "You are crying because you cannot see the food on your plate. There are people of the world who are crying because they have no food!"

When Albert finished this line, I immediately said to myself, "Aha! Who is blind here, Albert or me?"

Albert's story told me of my own blindness: blindness in the lack of appreciation for my own senses, blindness in my fear of being with "different" types of people, blindness in not trusting in God, blindness in not believing I could be given a lesson from a group of disabled people.

Returning home from that retreat, I stopped at a local supermarket and purchased some flowers as a symbol of Albert's story. Now whenever I am in a supermarket and see a small bouquet of flowers, they remind me of what I learned on that retreat day.

In the space provided write your "aha" experience story. When you are finished writing, summarize your experience by suggesting a sign or symbol that captures your lesson(s) from the "aha" experience.

Discovering

We have discovered that the "aha" experience reveals something about ourselves and our world. Indeed, Luke presents "aha" stories from which we can learn about ourselves and our relationship with God. Luke wishes us to see the awe and wonder of God through the Gospel accounts about Jesus. Through understanding Jesus' relationship with God, we will experience our relationship with God through Jesus. In listening and believing in Luke's stories of Jesus, we will discover the way to transform our lives in God.

The Gospel "aha" stories, then, become faith stories. In fact, this idea can be the foundation for an understanding of what the Bible truly is. The Bible is a book of faith, written by people of faith, to a community of faith. This faith is an experience of God.

Discovering

Now it is time for us to hear Luke's "aha" story of Jesus. For this first exercise you are asked to read Luke's Gospel in one sitting. If your schedule does not permit this, then you are encouraged to read Luke according to the divisions listed below. The importance here is that you read and hear the story. Just as it would be foolish for us to think we know a story without listening to it, it is foolish to think we can journey with Luke without reading the primary source: that is, the Gospel itself.

A few techniques may assist you in listening to the story. These techniques force you to slow the pace and train your ear to hear the story:

• Provide yourself the luxury of a quiet place and time to accomplish this task.
• Move your lips while reading, or read the Gospel aloud to yourself.
• Small groups should select one member to act as reader while the others listen, preferably without following along with their Bibles.

Read all of Luke in one sitting or according to these divisions:

• Luke 1:1—2:52*
• Luke 3:1—9:50
• Luke 9:51—19:27
• Luke 19:28—24:53

In the space provided write the key ideas and "aha" experiences you heard while listening to Luke's Gospel. *Remember, there is a diversity of responses.* Try to list three to ten items.

1)

2)

3)

4)

5)

6)

7)

8)

9)

10)

---

* In Gospel citations, the first number refers to the *chapter,* which is followed by a *colon,* and the next number lists the *verse* or *verses.* For example, Luke 9:51 is the ninth chapter, 51st verse of the Gospel of Luke.

Exploring

Listed are key "aha" experiences I have discovered from reading Luke's Gospel. Compare your list with mine. Some of these ideas will be the foundation for future Journeys:

• The Gospel is written to Theophilus.
• Mary plays a major role in the birth story of Jesus.
• At age twelve, Jesus speaks of being about his father's business.
• The Holy Spirit is often mentioned, especially when associated with prayer and action.
• There is a struggle between Jesus and the demons.
• The scribes and Pharisees are always questioning Jesus.
• There is a balance between stories concerning men and stories concerning women.
• The disciples are sent in teams of two.
• Many times only the Samaritans understand Jesus' mission and words.
• Jesus appears to the disciples after his Resurrection and up to the time of the Ascension.

Looking Back

On Journey 1 you made the following discoveries:

• Stories, especially "aha" stories, reveal something of ourselves and our place with creation.
• The Bible is a collection of faith stories—written by people of faith to a community of faith.
• It is important to read Luke's Gospel aloud in order to hear the story.
• It is important to list key ideas after reading Luke's Gospel.

For Further Exploration

Hall, T. William, Richard Pilgrim and Ronald Cavanagh. *Religion: An Introduction*. San Francisco, Calif.: Harper and Row Publishers, 1985.

Journey 2

Qualities of Luke's Writing

Most scholars agree that Luke is the author of both the Gospel and the Book of Acts. Luke thus provides a two-volume series which I have entitled: Volume I, "The Journey to God With Jesus" (Gospel), and Volume II, "The Journey to God With Jesus and the Church" (Acts). The two volumes present a universal message of salvation for all people, a point we will discover in Journey 3 when reviewing Simeon's prophecy (Luke 2:32).

Discovering

Let us review the universal message found in other sections of Luke's Gospel.
    Read Luke 3:6 and 24:47-48.

Exploring

In these two accounts we discover that "all mankind shall see the salvation of God" (Luke 3:6) which is "in his name...preached to all the nations, beginning at Jerusalem" (Luke 24:47).

Discovering

The reference to Jerusalem in Luke 24:47 is not merely to establish location. Jerusalem is symbolic of the place where one finds God. Throughout his Gospel, Luke will have us on a journey to Jerusalem. The journey to Jerusalem—on the way to finding God—is just as important as the destination itself, Jerusalem. Jerusalem is the final destination because that is where God is.

    This symbolic use of Jerusalem is similar to a vacation trip taken by my wife, Elizabeth, and me. The summer after we married, we traveled to the Northeast and Midwest sections of the country. The purpose was to celebrate our marriage with family and friends who could not witness the actual wedding ceremony. That summer, however, was not spent merely moving from one city to another. Rather, the entire summer was spent beginning our journey as husband and wife with the ultimate destination of being an example to the Christian community of what God expects of married people. At different spots along the way, we celebrated that journey with family and friends. Just as important as our traveling from one destination to another were the events and people along the way. We hope to continue the journey toward our destination throughout our lives. Just as in

Luke's Gospel, the endpoint of the journey is only important because of the things experienced along the way.

Discovering

Similar to other writers, Luke employs certain interesting techniques in presenting his two-volume series. By using the technique of parallelism, Luke is drawing on both the Gospel and Acts to complement each other and to provide one complete work.

    Read the following passages, first from the Gospel and then from Acts. (Example: read Luke 1:3-4 first, and then Acts 1:1.) Write a brief description under each citation of the action described in the account.

Gospel

Luke 1:3-4

Luke 3:22

Luke 5:17-26

Luke 7:11-17

Luke 22:66

Luke 23:4

Book of Acts

Acts 1:1

Acts 2:2-4

Acts 3:1-10

Acts 9:36-43

Acts 23:1

Acts 23:26-29

meaning.) This technique encourages the reader to discover the connection between Luke's two works. Notice that Luke 1:3-4 and Acts 1:1 are addressed to Theophilus, a familiar Greek name meaning *God's friend*. It is not clear from either the Gospel or Acts whether this is a real individual or a symbolic figure representing all believers or all God's friends. If we assume Luke is addressing his writing to all God's friends, then we can consider ourselves Theophilus.

Besides the parallelism found between the Gospel and Acts, Luke provides a parallelism within the Gospel itself. We will discover the parallelism within the Gospel when we deal with the birth stories of Luke 1 and 2 discovered in Journey 3.

Discovering

We can learn about other characteristics of Luke's writing at this time.

Read Luke 2:25-35 and Luke 2:36-38.
Read Luke 10:25-37 and Luke 10:38-41.
Read Luke 15:4-6 and Luke 15:8-9.

In the space provided answer the following question. What did you discover from these three pairs of accounts?

Exploring

By comparing the two citations, I have arrived at the following similarities:

- Luke 1:3-4 and Acts 1:1: written to Theophilus.
- Luke 3:22 and Acts 2:2-4: coming of the Holy Spirit.
- Luke 5:17-26 and Acts 3:1-10: curing of the paralytic.
- Luke 7:11-17 and Acts 9:36-43: raising of the dead to life.
- Luke 22:66 and Acts 23:1: coming of Jesus/Paul before the Council.
- Luke 23:4 and Acts 23:26-29: declaration of Jesus/Paul as innocent.

Discovering

The above samplings from the Gospel and Acts demonstrate the literary technique of parallelism common to Luke's work. (Parallel construction presents in a similar form ideas or expressions that are similar in content and

Exploring

These examples demonstrate the balance between stories involving men and stories involving women. It is this type of balance that underscores one of Luke's major themes: Salvation is offered to all.

Discovering

Besides the balance between men and women, there is also a kind of balance between Luke and the other Gospel writers, Mark and Matthew. Matthew, Mark and Luke are referred to as Synoptic Gospels. The term *synoptic* is a Greek word suggesting that one can place the three Gospels next to one another and generally get the same view of the material with one (syn) look (optic).

Read Luke 3:21-22.
Read Mark 1:9-11.
Read Matthew 3:13-17.

Exploring

Notice the similarity in these three accounts of the Baptism of Jesus. Scholars noticed other passages were also similar between the Synoptic writers. This similarity led to the theory that the Synoptic writers may have borrowed material from each other. The major theory claims Mark was the first writer, and Luke and Matthew borrowed from him. In the Introduction I compared Luke with Mark in order to date Luke's writing around A.D. 85.

Discovering

Scholars also noted that some material is common to both Luke and Matthew but not Mark. The following are two examples:
Read Luke 3:7-9 and Matthew 3:7-10.
Read Luke 6:20-24 and Matthew 5:3-12.

Exploring

From these examples and others, it appears Luke and Matthew shared an unknown source containing Jesus' sayings. In biblical study this unknown source is referred to as the Q source, from the German word *quelle* meaning source.

Discovering

A further comparison of the Synoptic material reveals that some stories are only common to a particular writer. For example, in Luke's Gospel there is an entire section of material, Luke 9:51—19:27, not included by the other Gospel writers.

Hence, the popular biblical theory is that Luke gathered his material from Mark, Q and his own sources. A common diagram used by biblical scholars to demonstrate this theory is:

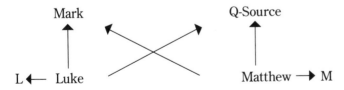

Discovering

Another kind of balance is created by the way the stories have been gathered and placed as a Gospel. In Journey 1 we defined the Bible as a book of faith, written by people of faith, to a community of faith. These experiences of faith were first shared orally. When it was feared the stories may be lost, they were collected and placed in written form. The author, when writing his Gospel, sifts through the stories, and selects and arranges those stories that say something about faith to his community. While stating something about faith to the community, the author is more interested in the central message of the story rather than reporting the *exact* words of the story.

Exact wording is difficult to capture when a story moves from one individual to another. It is even more difficult when the story is retold over a period of time. In the case of biblical writing, we assume Luke's writing to be around the year A.D. 85. This is approximately 52 years after Jesus' Resurrection when the stories were initially repeated by the disciples (Jesus' Resurrection is dated around the year A.D. 33 in our calendar). From the first rendition of the story until its final written form, scholars believe the story passes through three levels:
1) what Jesus actually said,
2) what the disciples preached about Jesus and his sayings, and
3) what was written about what Jesus said.

Jesus spent his years of ministry training his disciples and instructing them about the Kingdom. This is level one.

After Jesus' death and resurrection, the disciples preached the message of Jesus to their communities. The preaching was geared toward particular communities and was based on *remembrance* of Jesus' words, not his exact words. This is level two.

Then, a writer (such as Luke) saved the stories and preaching in written form. This is level three.

Discovering

Finally, Luke develops certain themes in his writing. Unlike the other Gospel writers whose Gospels can be separated into major sections, Luke designs a Gospel with interrelating themes found throughout his account. He is more concerned with allowing the material to speak for itself through these themes rather than offering one main thesis. Throughout the rest of our Journeys, we will review Luke's themes of joy, forgiveness, table ministry, the work of the Spirit, prayer, respect for women and justice.

Looking Back

On Journey 2 you made the following discoveries:

- the parallelism between Luke's Gospel and the Acts;
- the parallelism between Luke's Gospel and those of Mark and Matthew;
- the balance between stories of men and women;
- the theory that Luke in writing his Gospel used material

from Mark, Q and his own source;
• the interrelating themes in Luke's Gospel, rather than one main thesis, which allow the material to speak for itself;
• the idea that Gospel moves through three levels: (1) what Jesus said, (2) what was preached about what Jesus said and (3) what was written about what was preached about what Jesus said.

For Further Exploration

Flanagan, Neil. *Mark, Matthew and Luke: A Guide to the Gospel Parallels*. Collegeville, Minn.: The Liturgical Press, 1978.

Throckmorton, Burton H., ed. *Gospel Parallels: A Synopsis of the First Three Gospels*, rev. ed. Nashville, Tenn.: Thomas Nelson, Inc., 1979.

Journey 3
Infancy Narratives: Story of Births

Birth Stories

There is always something mysterious about the birth of a new child. Within our lives, some births are more miraculous than others. My sister, from the beginning of her marriage, realized that having children was going to be a difficulty due to a gynecological problem. The first five years of her marriage were spent praying and hoping some miracle would occur. There was great excitement when my sister announced she was expecting and even more excitement when she had her first child, Ricky. The family was overjoyed when a year later she had her second son, Edward. We could not believe it when three years later she had her third son, Robert. Upon the birth of her fourth son, Raymond, members of the family began thinking she had had enough children and her prayers were more than answered. However, the miracle occurred again with her fifth son, David, and the final miracle came with her daughter, Maura. Each of these births is a miracle unto itself because of my sister's medical problems. The birth of these children, however, is more than an overcoming of a medical difficulty; it is the celebration of life itself and the joy of a family.

Luke also presents a miracle story about a birth. His purpose is to relate the miracle of life rather than a biological happening. Just as there is a profound impact on my sister's and brother-in-law's lives with the births of their six children, there is a profound impact on all of our lives with God becoming human. Luke wants us to recognize the greatness of Jesus by sharing with us the greatness of his birth.

Discovering: Announcement Stories

Read Luke 1:5-38.

Place the sequence of events for the two announcement stories of the births of John and Jesus in the spaces provided. When listing events look for similarities between the two announcement stories.

Announcement of John's birth

Announcement of Jesus' birth

Exploring

Compare your listing with the listing provided.

Announcement of John's Birth		Announcement of Jesus' Birth
1:5-10	Naming of child's parents	1:26-27
1:11	Angel appears	1:28
1:12	Parent is disturbed by visit	1:29
1:13-17	Birth of child is announced	1:30-33
1:18-19	Question by parent and explanation	1:34-35
1:20	Sign	1:36-37
1:21-25	Conclusion	1:38

Discovering

The first event listed on page 11 introduces the parents of the children to be born. Beginning with the events of John's announcement, Luke informs us that Zechariah and Elizabeth were "just in the eyes of God, blamelessly following all the commandments..." (1:6). They are childless, however, which would make one wonder if they were really blessed by God. The childlessness of this couple is intensified by the fact that they are both advanced in years.

Read Genesis 12:1-3; Genesis 15; Genesis 17; Genesis 21:1-4.

Exploring

The rich story of Abraham and Sarah and the birth of their son, Isaac, is the background for the introduction to Zechariah and Elizabeth. Just as God blessed Abraham and Sarah in their old age, so now God will bless Zechariah and Elizabeth. Luke expects us to know the story of Abraham and Sarah and immediately see the connection between the two couples. (Despite the fact that Luke is writing to a Gentile community, scholars believe that Gentiles became skilled in the Old Testament in order to trace the prophecies concerning the coming of the Messiah.)

Zechariah is at prayer when the announcement comes from the angel. Throughout our Journeys, we will discover that prayer is a central theme to the Lucan message.

The core of the story is the announcement of the birth of John. Here we learn of the greatness of John and his mission. John is filled with the Spirit (another important Lucan theme) and is sent to convert Israel just as the prophet Elijah was. The importance of John to the Gospel message will be presented in Journey 4.

Discovering

The announcement by the Angel Gabriel reminds us of another Old Testament reference.

Read Daniel 9:20-27.

Exploring

The Book of Daniel is an example of apocalyptic writing style. (The Book of Revelation is an example of this style found in the New Testament.) This style is highly symbolic and often presented during times of great persecution. In this section of Daniel 9 reference is being made to a new age. Similarly, the Angel Gabriel in Luke 1:19 is announcing a new age in which John will act as a forerunner.

Discovering

Zechariah's reaction of disbelief is similar to Abraham's reaction (Genesis 17:17). Zechariah becomes speechless as a result of his disbelief. This speechlessness becomes a sign because it points to the workings of God. This sign is similar to an account presented in Daniel 10:15-18 which also tells of a person speechless and powerless.

With this background information, it is helpful to reflect on the entire image presented by the announcement of John's birth and the emphasis on Zechariah. In the space provided write one or two sentences that summarize the picture presented in this Lucan account.

Exploring

Luke, in the imagery of Zechariah, presents the end of the Old Testament message and announces a new age. This new age will be brought about by John the Baptist who is the Elijah-figure coming to announce the Messiah.

Discovering

We now focus our attention on the announcement story of the birth of Jesus and notice the connection between the two birth stories. Just as we were introduced to the childless parents of John, we are introduced to Mary and Joseph who are childless because of not yet being married. The announcement of the birth and a new age is made by the Angel Gabriel. Here again we can refer to the Book of Daniel and the coming of a new age. And, the sign, Mary's cousin Elizabeth being with child, points to the wonderful acts of God.

Exploring

Although there is a parallelism between these two announcement stories, there are also major differences:

- John is conceived by parents who are barren and elderly; Jesus is conceived by a virgin.
- Faithful to Old Testament tradition and its patriarchal emphasis, Zechariah is the key figure in the John story and not Elizabeth. Mary, not Joseph, however, is important in the announcement of Jesus' birth.
- John's conception comes through God's overcoming a human inability to conceive; Jesus' conception is solely the work of God.
- John is *filled* with the Spirit; Jesus is *conceived* by the Spirit.

Discovering

Just as you summarized the imagery presented in John's story, write your reflection on the announcement story of Jesus' birth and the role of Mary.

Exploring

Mary represents all Christians who must be willing to allow Christ to be conceived in them.

Discovering: The Visitation

Read Luke 1:39-56.

Reflect on the imagery presented in this scene of Mary's visit to Elizabeth. In the space provided write a brief paragraph that best highlights your insights from reading these passages.

Exploring

- Mary's visit to Elizabeth allows for the encounter of Jesus and John.
- It is Elizabeth, as well as John, who is filled with the Spirit as a result of this visit.
- It is only because of Jesus that John is great.
- Elizabeth realizes the greatness of God through the visit of the "mother of my Lord..." (1:43).

Discovering

Scholars in working with the Visitation story make reference to Elizabeth and Mary being symbolic of the Old and New Testament. Mary (New Testament) coming to visit Elizabeth (Old Testament) demonstrates the fulfillment of the Old Testament is found in Christ (New Testament). Mary has been portrayed as the model of the Church that is to bring forth the Christ. Here, in this comparison, we see she is also the bridge between the Old and New Testament since in her delivery of Jesus the New Testament age begins.

Mary's reaction to all of this is her canticle.
Read I Samuel 2:1-10.

Exploring

The inspiration for Mary's canticle is taken from Hannah's song of I Samuel. In this canticle we receive a preview of some themes found in Luke's Gospel, especially verses 51-53.

Discovering: Birth Stories

Read the following accounts: Luke 1:57-80 and Luke 2:1-40. Under the columns provided, write the similarities discovered between the birth of John and the birth of Jesus.

John's birth   **Jesus' birth**

Exploring

Compare your similarities with mine.

John's Birth   **Jesus' Birth**

1:57	Child's birth	2:1-7
1:58	Rejoicing at birth	2:8-20
1:59	Circumcision of child	2:21
1:60-66	Greatness of child	2:22-28
1:67-79	Canticle	2:29-38
1:80	Development of child	2:39-40

The account of John's birth introduces two major themes found in Luke's Gospel. The first is joy, which is highlighted by the reaction of Elizabeth's neighbors and relatives (1:58). The second is the idea of sign, which points to the workings of God:

- The return of Zechariah's ability to speak is a sign of God's mercy, thus causing Zechariah to praise God.
- The fear that descended on all in the neighborhood is a sign of the mighty acts of God.
- John will become a sign since the hand of the Lord is upon him.

- With all of these signs and with the great news of John's birth and mission, the response by Zechariah is to sing. Notice the prophecy is uttered under the influence of the Spirit.
- Typical of Old Testament prayer, Zechariah begins with a song of thanksgiving (1:68-70).
- The salvific and merciful acts of God are praised (1:71-75). Zechariah's reference to the great covenant with Abraham can be found in Genesis 15 and Genesis 17.
- Speaking to his child, Zechariah sings of the mission of John the Baptist who is the forerunner of the Most High (1:76-77).
- Zechariah's conclusion is on the mercy of God—a God who is the Dayspring (light). This emphasis on light comes from the Old Testament references of Isaiah 60:1 and Malachi 3:20. The New Testament emphasis is going to come from Luke who wants us to see Jesus as light for all humankind.

Discovering: The Birth of Jesus

Although there is a parallel between the story of the birth of John and the story of the birth of Jesus, the greatest emphasis is naturally on the birth of Jesus. It may be helpful to our study to reflect on the broad images presented in the birth story of Jesus rather than every detail.

In the space provided write your responses to the following questions:

1) What is Luke attempting to say to his readers with his emphasis on "first-born son"?

2) What image is presented by Jesus being wrapped in swaddling clothes?

3) What is the image of laying Jesus in a manger?

4) What is Luke attempting to say by painting a scene of no room in the inn?

Exploring

Compare your responses with mine.

1) The emphasis on "first-born son" refers us to the great status of the first child receiving the birthright and the father's blessing. Its intention is not to make reference to the birth order of siblings. The Old Testament story of Esau and Jacob (Genesis 25 and 27) provides further insight to this theme of birthright and blessing. The line is clarified when translated: "to a son, the first born." It is Christ, the firstborn of all humanity, who will make possible God's blessing on all.

2) To swaddle a child is to demonstrate love and nurturing. Three ideas may be reflected upon regarding the swaddling.

- In light of the background of the great leaders of the Roman Empire (2:1-5), Christ is born in poverty and is the true ruler of all.
- The swaddling of the child hints to the crucified Christ who will be wrapped in linen cloth (23:53).
- Reference is to the Book of Wisdom:

   "In swaddling clothes and with
      constant care I was nurtured.
   For no king has any different origin or birth,
      but one is the entry into life for all;
   and in one same way they leave it."
   (Wisdom 7:4-6)

The emphasis here is on the kingship of Jesus rather than on a poor state in life.

3) A manger is obviously a trough to which animals come to eat. The Lucan Gospel refers to the manger in 2:7, 2:12 and 2:16, a hint that the manger may be symbolic or at least important for Luke since it is mentioned three times. Christ being placed in the manger can be a symbol that he is food for all. This may also be a Eucharistic reference with ties to other Lucan passages that have table fellowship (Eucharist) as a major theme.

4) The image presented of "no room for them…" (Luke 2:7) could have been due to conditions surrounding a census. However, customs surrounding the Middle East lead us to believe that it would be inhospitable and unthinkable for people not to have some room. When we emphasize that there was no room for *them*, we understand the problem. On reflection, we know what it is like when there is no room for us, but there may be room for others. In this imagery, we receive a hint that Jesus will not be accepted by all and for some there is no room for him in their life.

Discovering

The result of the birth of Jesus is joy: a joy demonstrated by the angels, shepherds, Simeon and Anna. The joy of the shepherds and Luke's emphasis on their adoration of the Christ Child acclaims the fact that Christ has come for all. During this time, shepherds were viewed as outcasts. Luke will make continuous reference to Christ's coming for the alienated throughout his Gospel.

The rejoicing songs of Simeon and Anna demonstrate the balance between male and female so often found in the Lucan Gospel. Simeon's song also signals the greatness of God. It is Simeon (filled with the Spirit) who announces that Christ is the saving deed (salvation) for all. It is from Simeon's prayer that we are introduced to the overall message of Luke's Gospel: Christ is "a revealing light to the Gentiles" (2:32). His prayer is immediately followed by Anna's thanksgiving prayer.

Discovering: Finding Jesus in the Temple

Working with the rich imagery of this section on the Infancy Narratives encourages us to read other accounts and look for the imagery presented. We discovered the imagery surrounding Mary as the Mother of God who bridges the Old and New Testament. We discovered the imagery surrounding the manger as a symbol of Christ being food for all. We discovered the imagery of the song of Zechariah as a sign of God's greatness.

Searching for the imagery in an account allows us to view the passages with biblical ears and eyes. With our ears and eyes attuned to the richness of the account, we begin to *hear* and to *see* in a different way. When a writer repeats a particular word or setting, he is asking us to pay special note. An example is the triple reference to *manger*.

Another example is the way Luke uses the idea of the Spirit. Thus far, we have learned that it is the working of the Spirit that brings about so many happenings.

In this section you are asked to read an account with biblical ears and eyes. The intention is to get beyond the literal and to see if the writer is asking you to make a theological connection.

Read Luke 2:41-50.

In the space provided and using biblical ears and eyes, what theological insight have you gained from this passage? (Hint: You may want to begin with key words or concepts.)

Exploring

In reading this account I notice four key concepts: (a) the Passover feast, (b) Jesus is lost, (c) his parents search for him for three days and (d) Jesus "had" to be in his Father's house.

The first three concepts parallel the passion, death and resurrection of Jesus. During the Passover feast, he will be crucified, placed in a tomb and will rise on the third day. The passion, death and resurrection are part of Jesus' mission to serve the Father. This point corresponds to the fourth key concept of Jesus having to be in his Father's house.

Looking Back

On Journey 3 you made the following discoveries:

- the key elements of the birth announcement stories of both John and Jesus;
- the Old Testament parallels to Zechariah, Elizabeth and Mary's canticle;
- the importance of Mary as a bridge between the Old and New Testaments;
- the major elements in the birth story of Jesus;
- the importance of studying a biblical passage with biblical eyes and ears;
- the connection between Jesus being found in the Temple and the passion, death and resurrection of Jesus.

For Further Exploration

Brown, Raymond E. *The Birth of The Messiah*. Garden City, N.Y.: Doubleday & Company, 1977.

Journey 4
Another Beginning

The invitation to the party for my fortieth birthday read as follows:

> In the Spring of '43
> Pius XII was Bishop of Rome,
> Franklin Delano Roosevelt was President of the United States.
> The New York Yankees were on their way to winning the World Series.
> *Oklahoma!* was opening on Broadway,
> and Rosalie and Eddie Apicella gave birth to their third child, Raymond.

From a global perspective, it is rather presumptuous to place my birth in light of these people and events. But, from a personal view, it suggests my birth is as important for me and my friends as these events.

Discovering

Luke, in the beginning of Chapter 3 of the Gospel, offers a similar comparison of events with the start of Jesus' ministry and the political and religious situation of the time. Although the actual beginning of Luke's Gospel is found in Chapters 1 and 2 with the annunciation, visitation and birth stories of both John the Baptist and Jesus (see Journey 3), many scholars suggest that Luke's Gospel actually begins with Chapter 3.

Read Luke 3:1-6.

In the following citations from the Old Testament, notice the similarity between the Old Testament passages and Luke's beginning of Chapter 3.

Read Hosea 1:1.
Read Amos 1:1.

Exploring

The Old Testament passages—as does Luke 3—place a particular event in terms of the political and religious leadership of the time. This style is a common technique found among Greek writers of the time. Its intention is not merely to provide historical dating, but rather to have the reader connect the start of Jesus' ministry with the prophetic writings of the Old Testament.

Some historical background information regarding individuals mentioned in Luke 3 provides additional information for our study.

• Tiberius, the second emperor of the Roman Empire, began his reign around A.D. 14. The mention of his fifteenth year of reign (around A.D. 28-29) has been used by some scholars to date the activities of Jesus.

• Herod Tetrarch of Galilee, the son of Herod the Great, reigned from around 4 B.C.E. to A.D. 39. Therefore, all of Jesus' life was lived under his reign.

• Philip and Lysanias were tetrarchs (governors) of the other sections of the kingdom. In 3:1 Luke gives the historical division of the kingdom, which belonged initially to Herod the Great.

• In Luke 3:2 Luke introduces two high priests, Annas and Caiaphas. Never in the religious history of Israel were there two high priests. Placing both together, however, Luke suggests that Caiaphas, the son-in-law of Annas and the current high priest, was influenced by his father-in-law.

Discovering

With the Roman political and Jewish religious situations as background, Luke presents John the Baptist. John, acting as the forerunner of Jesus, is the one who will prepare the way for the "true" leader and the "true" priest, Jesus.

Discovering: John the Baptist

Luke's treatment of John in the infancy narratives (Luke 1 and 2) suggests he is an important figure to the Gospel account. As background material, you must remember John is the one of whom Jesus claims, "I assure you, there is no man born of woman greater than John" (Luke 7:28).

Read Luke 1:14-17.

In the space provided summarize in your own words the angel's message about John the Baptist.

Exploring

In verses 14-17 we observe the message concerning John's way of life, which is to never drink wine or strong drink (1:15). We also see John's mission, which is to bring many back to God (1:16), and to act in the spirit of Elijah (1:17), which is to prepare for the Lord (1:17).

Discovering

Read the following verses from Malachi in the order presented for you.

Malachi 3:23
Malachi 1:1-5

Summarize in your own words the information received from Malachi.

Exploring

Malachi teaches that Elijah will come before the Lord to prepare the way. This is the Elijah from II Kings 2:11 who was taken to heaven in a fiery chariot. His preparation will prepare the way for the Lord to come as the divine judge.

Discovering

Read Luke 3:3-6.

John is now the Elijah figure preparing the way for the Lord. The Isaiah quote (Isaiah 40:3-5) comes from a time when the role of a predecessor was to enter before the king in order to prepare the roads for the king's arrival. John is the preparer for Jesus. John's instruction, however, is not to prepare externally (as for a road), but to prepare internally, our hearts, for the coming of Christ.

Read Luke 3:7-21.

List in your own words the key points of John's message.

Exploring

John acts as a prophet and his message is not all that comforting, just as the prophets' message was not one of comforting but rather an exhortation to bring one's heart back to God.

- Luke 3:7-9. John calls for a reform. No longer can individuals rest on the faith of their ancestors but on how they live out their own lives.
- Luke 3:10-11. We cannot be selfish but must care for all people.
- Luke 3:12-13. Tax collectors, who were known to extort monies from people for personal use, must stop abusing their role.
- Luke 3:15-16. John realizes his own shortcomings in comparison to Jesus.
- Luke 3:17. John paints a judgment theme that suggests Jesus will separate the good (wheat) from the evil (chaff).

The key points highlighted from this passage place emphasis on John's prophetic role (like Elijah) rather than his baptizing role. Notice that John is already arrested by Herod (3:19-20) before the Baptism of Jesus takes place (3:21-22).

Looking Back

On Journey 4 you made the following discoveries:

- Most scholars believe Luke 3 is the actual beginning of the Gospel.
- Luke places the ministry of Jesus within the political and religious background of the time.
- Luke's writing style found in 3:1ff is a popular technique used by Greek writers and is comparable to what is found in prophetic books of the Old Testament.
- John the Baptist is the Elijah figure who has come to prepare the way of the Lord.

For Further Exploration

Fitzmyer, Joseph A. *The Gospel According to Luke (I-IX)*, Anchor Bible Series. Garden City, N.Y.: Doubleday & Company, Inc., 1981.

Schweizer, Eduard. *The Good News According to Luke*. Atlanta, Ga.: John Knox Press, 1984.

Journey 5
The Spirit

Luke, more than any other Gospel writer, presents the Spirit as key to understanding Jesus' mission. It is Jesus, filled with the Spirit, who is revealing God's message. We have been introduced to the Spirit's power in our studies of the infancy narratives (Journey 3).

Discovering

In Journey 4 we ended with John's arrest and Jesus' Baptism. In this Journey, we will investigate the importance of this baptismal scene and the importance of the Spirit.

Read Luke 3:21-22.

In the space provided record each sequence of events found in the passages of Jesus' Baptism:

Exploring

The sequence of events is as follows:

- All people have been baptized.
- Jesus is at prayer after being baptized.
- The skies open.
- The Holy Spirit descends on Jesus like a dove.
- A voice proclaims Jesus as the beloved Son on whom God's favor rests.

Discovering

Notice this listing of events does not place emphasis on the Baptism itself, but rather the events after the Baptism. The scene begins with Jesus at prayer followed by the sky opening and the Spirit coming. The connection between prayer and the Spirit is paramount for Luke.

Read the following verses:

Luke 5:16
Luke 6:12
Luke 9:18
Luke 9:28
Luke 11:1
Luke 22:32
Luke 22:39-46
Luke 23:46

Exploring

In each of these passages we notice the common reference to Jesus at prayer. Within this Journey and future Journeys, we will be reminded of the connection between prayer and the Spirit. Remember it was when Zechariah was at prayer that the angel came, and it was when Mary was at prayer that the angel announced she was to be the Mother of God.

Discovering

In the baptismal scene of Jesus a major event is the sky opening and the Spirit descending in the image of a dove. This image of opening sky and descending dove is rooted in the Old Testament. In Isaiah 63:19b we read: "Oh, that you would rend the heavens and come down...." A similar imagery is given in Ezekiel 1:1. In Ezekiel 2:2 there is reference to spirit entering the prophet. The image of the Spirit as a dove can be traced to Genesis 1:2 where the Spirit of God ("mighty wind") hovers over the waters of creation.

Discovering

Read Isaiah 42:1.

In the space provided write the similarities you discover between this passage from Isaiah and Jesus' baptismal scene as described in Luke.

Exploring

The reference to the prophet being "my chosen one with whom I am pleased" (Isaiah 42:1a) is similar to "You are my beloved Son. On you my favor rests" (Luke 3:22b).

Discovering

Luke's Gospel makes numerous other references to the Spirit. Read each of the following verses and in the space provided, paraphrase each of these verses in your own words:

Luke 3:22

Luke 4:1

Luke 4:14

Luke 4:18

Luke 10:21

Luke 11:13

Luke 12:12

Luke 24:49

Exploring

From working with the passages, the following ideas unfold:

- Jesus is the man of the Spirit (3:22; 4:1; 4:14; 4:18; 10:21).
- The Holy Spirit is given to all who ask (11:13).
- The Holy Spirit is the one who teaches us (12:12).
- Jesus will send the promise of the Father and clothe us with power that is the Spirit (24:49).
- Although you did not read sources other than Gospel citations, it is understood that when one is clothed with the power of the Spirit, the work of the Church begins. This is the main theme found in the Book of Acts.

Discovering

The preceding passages referring to the Spirit and to prayer demonstrate the connection between the two. However, this prayer and the coming of the Spirit has a particular purpose: that is, to carry on the mission of the Gospel. Notice the references to Jesus being a man of the Spirit (3:22; 4:1; 4:14, etc.). Luke 4:14 is the first verse of the Gospel section subtitled, "The Ministry in Galilee." Jesus is the person of prayer who is filled with the Spirit in order to carry out his ministry: the mission of the Father. This anointing of the Father makes Jesus the one to bring glad tidings to the poor, to proclaim liberty to captives, to restore sight to the blind, to release prisoners and to announce a year of favor from the Lord (4:18-19).

Luke reminds us that, like Christ, we are to be people of prayer (11:13). As people of prayer, we are then recipients of the Spirit who will clothe us (24:49) and teach us (12:12) as to our mission and ministry for the Church.

Discovering: Scripture and the Contemporary Reader

Luke establishes Jesus as a man of prayer who is filled with the Spirit. His intention of presenting Jesus in such a manner is to provide us with an example. If Jesus is a man of prayer, so must we be people of prayer. If Jesus is filled with the Spirit, so must we plead for the Spirit to fill our lives. Prayer and the Spirit are essential to the Christian faith. Luke presents these lessons so we may grow in the faith. The encouragement to grow in faith lies at the center of biblical study.

The study of the Bible in general and Luke specifically is a matter of faith study rather than of historical and scientific documentation. It is true that historical background into the community of Luke is important to biblical knowledge as are the theological insights provided by biblical scholars. However, these insights acquired from history and theology are not the replacement for a deeper living out of a relationship with Jesus. As contemporary readers of Scripture, we must continually call upon the Spirit to open our minds and hearts to the gospel message so that we may be transformed into true followers of Christ.

The reflective exercises presented here and elsewhere in this manual are designed to force us to reflect on the essential message of the Gospel; that is, to reflect on the message God has for us. The techniques listed are mere aids to assist you with the meditation. You are encouraged to read through the entire exercise first and then, once comfortable with the suggested techniques, begin the reflective exercise.

Discovering

- Find a quiet place free from distraction. You may need thirty to forty-five minutes to complete this exercise.

- Have the necessary equipment available at the beginning of the meditation period so you can eliminate distractions. For this exercise, you will need your Bible, pencil or pen.
- Begin with a relaxing exercise of concentrating on your breathing. Try to be conscious of every breath entering your body as breaths of peace and joy. While exhaling, let yourself imagine anxiety and tension leaving your body.
- Read slowly the following prayer to the Spirit, which can be traced to the twelfth century:

Come Holy Spirit.
Fill the hearts of your faithful and make the fire of your love burn within them.
Send forth your spirit and there shall be a new creation.
And you shall renew the face of the earth.
O God, You have instructed the hearts of the faithful by the light of the Holy Spirit. Grant that through the same Holy Spirit, we may always be truly wise and rejoice in his consolation. Through Christ our Lord. Amen.

Discovering

Using the ancient prayer as background, reflect on some ideas from Luke.

- *Come Holy Spirit.* Reflect on Luke 10:21.
- *Fill the hearts of your faithful.* Reflect on Luke 24:30-32.
- *Send forth your Spirit.* Reflect on Luke 21:15.
- *And there shall be another creation.* Reflect on Luke 12:32-34.
- *And you shall renew the face of the earth.* Reflect on Luke 6:27-36.

In the space provided write your responses to the following questions:

1) In what areas do I need to ask the Spirit to come into my life?

2) What actions do I need to consider that will demonstrate my desire to be faithful?

3) How can I bring about a new creation in my life and the lives of others?

4) What deeds must I perform to renew the face of the earth?

Looking Back

On Journey 5 you made the following discoveries:

- One of Luke's major themes is on the Spirit.
- The baptismal scene of Jesus is rooted in Old Testament accounts.
- There is a definite link between prayer, the Spirit and performing the work of the Church.
- The pattern of prayer, the Spirit and action is something we must reflect on within our lives.
- There are certain techniques that can assist us in our desire as contemporary biblical scholars to blend the mind and heart.

For Further Exploration

Alday, Carrillo Salvador. *Power From on High: The Holy Spirit in the Gospels and Acts*. Ann Arbor, Mich.: Servant Books, 1978.

Apicella, Raymond. *Journeys Into Mark: 16 Lessons of Exploration and Discovery*. Cincinnati, Ohio: St. Anthony Messenger Press, 1990.

LaVerdiere, Eugene. *Luke*. New Testament Message, Vol. 5. Wilmington, Del.: Michael Glazier, Inc., 1983.

Journey 6

Discipleship in Luke, Part One: Mission and Requirements

During the historical time of Jesus, it was not uncommon for a person to leave family and friends to follow a popular leader. The disciple attaches to the individual, who serves as mentor in guiding the individual along a particular practice or life-style.

Discovering

Jesus did not initiate this practice of discipleship but did invite followers to learn his way and follow his life-style. In Luke's Gospel the disciple is called to follow Jesus on his journey to God.

Read Luke 5:1-11.

In this call of Peter and Zebedee's sons write the response of the disciples to the call from Jesus.

Exploring

The disciples' responses may be listed as following:

- Peter admits his sinfulness (5:8).
- They (Peter, James, John) leave everything to follow (5:11).

Discovering

Read Luke 5:27-28.

Similar to the initial call of Peter, Levi is willing to leave everything (5:28).

The disciples' response "to leave everything" is mentioned again in Luke 9:57-62.

Discovering

Read Luke 9:57-62.

The New American Bible subtitles this passage as "The Apostles' Requirements." The point of the passage is not simply to say good-bye to friends and family. Rather, the passage explains the reason for leaving what one knows in order to follow a new path. This new path presents a new mission—a new direction—that will be entirely different from that prior to the call.

Discovering

The "not looking back" (9:62) is a reprimand for not seeking the distractions of the past. It is rooted in the Old Testament story of the Exodus event. Once the Israelites were delivered from slavery and on the way to the promised land, they began complaining about their new situation. They longed for the "fleshpots of Egypt," which symbolized their longing for slavery and domination under the Pharaoh (Exodus 16:3).

Exploring

Reflecting on the connection between the Old Testament reprimand of not looking back and Peter's admittance of his sinfulness, Luke presents the beginning characteristics of discipleship.

- Discipleship is a call to the individual. It is pure gift. Peter, like the Israelites, was chosen by God and did nothing to deserve the call.
- Discipleship is a call from the known to the unknown. Peter is aware of what it means to be a fisherman. He has no awareness of what it means to be a disciple of Christ. The Israelites knew the condition of slavery under Pharaoh, but they had no awareness of what was ahead for them in the promised land. The movement to the unknown is always frightening; disciples must resist the temptation to return to previous ways especially when they realize how sinful their past behavior was.

Discovering

Read Luke 8:19-21.

In the space provided write what you learned about discipleship from this passage.

Exploring

The true disciple is one who hears the word of God and acts upon it (8:21).

Discovering

God's word for the disciple to hear is presented by Luke in "The Great Discourse" (Luke 6:20-26). This discourse by Christ is paralleled to another discourse presented by Moses, who gives the Ten Commandments (Exodus 20). Jesus has called his disciples (who represent the New Israel) and is ready to give them the word of God.

Read Luke 6:20-26.

In the space provided write your understanding of the four blessings and the four woes presented by Luke.

Blest are you poor....

Blest are you who hunger....

Blest are you who are weeping....

Blest are those hated....

Woe to you rich....

Woe to you who are full....

Woe to you who laugh....

Woe to you when all speak well....

Exploring

Compare your summations with mine.

Blest are you poor.... Luke's concern is for the alienated who are economically deprived and politically threatened. Such a situation does not allow people the right to chart their own destinies. The poor in this sense realize a dependency on God and not on things. It is God who creates the person and gives the person life. Realizing this great gift from God, the person is humbled.

Blest are you who hunger.... Hunger is an obvious result of poverty. However, there is a basic human drive for food and drink. This blessing suggests something more than the basic drive for food and drink; that is, a desire to fill one's hunger for God.

Blest are you who are weeping.... Realize that the life of discipleship may be one of pain. The disciple also realizes his/her previous life may not have always been filled with God. For that past time when relationship with God was not important, the disciple is sorry.

Blest are those hated.... Placing God as the center of one's life is a movement toward truth and away from sin and evil. Those who love chaos will resent the disciple for acting as God wants; thus, they will do everything to destroy the disciple.

Woe to you rich.... A warning is issued to those who create systems and conditions that imprison other people, and a deeper warning to those who do not have God at the center of their hearts.

Woe to you who are full.... A warning is given to those who place their trust in things and do not wish to be filled with God.

Woe to you who laugh.... A warning is given to those who do nothing to continue a relationship with God.

Woe to you when all speak well.... A warning is issued to those who attempt to compromise the word of God and refuse the challenge of the gospel message.

Discovering

Luke supplies additional insights for hearing the word of God and acting upon that word in Chapter 6. He will unfold some of these ideas in future Gospel accounts, and we will study some of these ideas in future Journeys. For now, it may be beneficial to read this account in a meditative mode. Before reading the remainder of Luke 6, practice the following techniques:

- Place yourself in a relaxed position with your Bible on your lap.
- Read aloud or move your lips while reading.
- Read slowly, pausing after ideas or thoughts that capture your heart.

- Do not be concerned if you do not finish the entire reading in one sitting. You may return to this section for further meditation and prayer.

Read Luke 6:27-49. Follow the techniques provided above for reflective reading.

Discovering

Luke warns his readers of the dangers of wealth. Therefore, it is necessary for us to seek some clarification on Luke's interpretation of poverty or "leaving all behind."

Read Luke 12:13-21; 32-34.

The difficulty of the man with the good harvest is not prosperity. Rather, his difficulty stems from his contentment in believing he can now relax because he has stored up treasure (12:19). He is foolish because his treasure can easily be lost due to death or destruction. The treasure of his heart is not God's word but things (12:34). This story encapsulates the blessings and warnings presented in Luke 6.

Discovering

For Luke, however, the problem is not wealth alone since Luke presents another story of the wealthy man, Zacchaeus (19:1-10). In this story Zacchaeus does not rely on materialism only, but lives an honest life in his relationship with others. Because of Zacchaeus' desire to act on the word of God, "salvation has come to this house..." (19:9).

Compare Luke 19:1-10 with Luke 18:18-30. Write the difference(s) you discover between Zacchaeus and the rich young man.

Exploring

- The rich young man can recite the law; Zacchaeus, however, lives the law.
- The rich young man grew melancholy (18:23), while Zacchaeus stood his ground (19:8).
- The story of Zacchaeus ends with the purpose of the Son of God. The story of the rich young man ends with a further lesson on the dangers of riches (18:24-25) and the benefits of leaving everything (18:29-30).

Discovering

Again Luke presents the theme of leaving everything. This lesson is something that cannot be ignored by the disciple. The challenge for the disciple is to be like Zacchaeus who has placed material wealth in its proper perspective. Quite simply, the disciple is faced with the difficult question: Who is the God of my heart? Is it greed, possessions or materialism? Or, is it God, Yahweh, to whom I am journeying with Jesus?

Read Luke 8:1-3.

What do you learn of discipleship from this account?

Exploring

This account emphasizes the women who were "assisting them out of their means" (8:3). Discipleship is a serving of others with the gifts one possesses. It is a willingness to serve so that the word of God can be proclaimed.

Discipleship is not a call for the individual to take care of self but a call to serve.

Discovering

Read Luke 10:1-17.

In the space provided list the circumstances and characteristics of disciples and their mission.

Exploring

Compare your listing with mine.

- Disciples are sent in pairs (10:1).
- Disciples are sent to hostile places (10:3).
- Disciples should not burden themselves with numerous possessions (10:4).
- Disciples should seek out supportive people (10:6).
- Disciples are to proclaim the word of God (10:9).
- Disciples are to leave places where they are not welcomed (10:10-15).
- Disciples are sent by Jesus (10:16).
- Disciples have power over Satan (10:17-19).
- Disciples will be given a true reward (10:20).

Discovering

Similar to the other Gospel writers, Luke continues to caution his readers who have chosen the road of discipleship.

Read Luke 9:23-27.

Exploring

In the call to serving God and others the disciple will meet hardship. Following the path of Jesus will include passion and death. The irony of this suffering, however, is that this death is not a spiritual death, but rather a death that brings life and resurrection.

Looking Back

On this Journey you discovered the following ideas on discipleship:

- Discipleship is forgiveness of sin and a willingness to give up all.
- Discipleship calls one to announce the word of God and not turn back.
- Disciples know who is the God of their hearts.
- Disciples have a particular mission.
- Disciples are called to serve others.
- Discipleship is a call to death that brings life.

For Further Exploration

Guinan, Michael. *Gospel Poverty: Witness to the Risen Christ.* Ramsey, N.J.: Paulist Press, 1981.

LaVerdiere, Eugene. *Luke.* Wilmington, Del.: Michael Glazier, Inc., 1980.

Schottroff, Luise, and Wolfgang Stegemann. *Jesus and the Hope of the Poor.* Maryknoll, N.Y.: Orbis Books, 1986.

Journey 7

Discipleship, Part Two: Neighbor and Hospitality

The previous Journey on discipleship unfolds ideas of mission, condition and requirements. In this Journey we further examine the concept of discipleship through the ideas of neighbor and hospitality. Luke addresses these concepts of discipleship by answering the question "What must I do to inherit everlasting life?" in the accounts of the Good Samaritan, and Martha and Mary. In these two accounts we discover a writing technique frequently found in Luke's Gospel. Often Luke begins his story with a *question* by one who should know the answer. The *response* comes in the form of a story, which itself forces the questioner to arrive at the answer; and finally comes a lesson, which contains examples for *application*.

Discovery

Read Luke 10:25-11:13.

In the space provided locate examples of the Lucan technique of question, response, application.

Exploring

Compare your answers with mine.

- The question—Luke 10:25; 29.
- The response in story form—Luke 10:30-37.
- The application—Luke 10:38-41.
- A question—Luke 11:1.
- The response—Luke 11:2-4.
- The application—Luke 11:5-13.

Discovering

Focusing our attention on the accounts of the Good Samaritan, and Martha and Mary, we notice the lesson begins with the question from a lawyer (10:25). The question is elementary since every lawyer would already know the law, central to the Old Testament writings.

Read Deuteronomy 6:5 and Leviticus 19:18.

Discovering

The lawyer does not stop his questioning but attempts to trick Jesus by asking, "And who is my neighbor?" (10:29). Typical of Jesus, his response is not a direct reply but rather a story.

The story immediately places the listener in a familiar setting: the road from Jerusalem to Jerico. This area is known as a desolate place and a haven for robbers to entrap their victims. One would not be surprised that the character of the story "fell prey to robbers" (10:30).

Likewise, the lawyer would not think it strange that both the priest and the Levite avoid this man who is now half dead or appears as dead. The victim is unclean and these two people of the law would be compelled to deal with the purification rites as outlined in Leviticus 12—15.

The introduction of the third character, the Samaritan, causes the lawyer difficulties. Samaritans were despised by the Jews. The historian, Josephus, relates the Samaritan's desecrating act of scattering dead bones throughout the Jerusalem Temple as just one account of the many wedges that separated these people. From approximately 128 B.C.E., the hostility between Jew and Samaritan had grown deeper and deeper.

The Samaritan, however, acts as a neighbor. His actions are recognized as neighborly by the lawyer.

The noted Scripture scholar, Eugene LaVerdiere, points out that the lawyer is still having difficulty. LaVerdiere claims the lawyer, who can only refer to the man as "the one," is an example of such a hatred that the word (in this case, *Samaritan*) cannot be pronounced.

The question, "And who is my neighbor?," forces the individual to examine the question from two points of view. From the lawyer's perspective, a neighbor is one closest in practices and beliefs. The priest and Levite would be his neighbors since they know and follow the law. From this viewpoint, the responsibility of neighbor is on the other person.

Luke, however, wishes us to see neighbor from the other point of view; that is, what does it mean for *me* to be a neighbor? This question is illustrated by the Samaritan who realizes that acting neighborly is taking care of others. This concern for others goes beyond those we know and like even to our enemies. Again for Luke, it goes to all people, especially the alienated.

Discovering

Another Samaritan story appears in Luke.

Read Luke 17:11-19.

Just as the first story is about a Good Samaritan who is a neighbor, this story depicts a Samaritan as one who is thankful to God and praises Jesus.

In the Introduction reference was made to Luke writing to a community associated with the evangelist Paul, responsible for the conversion of many Gentiles to Christianity. Likewise, in Journey 3, we discovered Luke's theme as Jesus is salvation for all. His placement of Samaritans as those who truly understand the gospel message may be a lesson for his community to continue with their efforts of evangelization to all people. Just as the Jewish lawyer could not believe in the Samaritan, those whom we least likely expect to follow the word of God may become the true believers.

Discovering

Read Luke 10:38-41.

Although not directly linked to the Good Samaritan account by story line, the story of Martha and Mary is connected by its placement in the same chapter. (It is further linked by recognizing the balance between stories of men and women in the Lucan Gospel.) Therefore, we can study this account as another response to the question, "What must I do to inherit everlasting life?" (10:25).

To formulate a response to the question, list below the key ideas of the story.

Exploring

Compare your list with mine.

- Jesus is on the journey with others.
- Martha welcomes Jesus into her home (hospitality).
- Mary is at the feet of Jesus.

- Martha is busy with the details of hospitality and complains about her sister's lack of help.
- Jesus chastises Martha about her anxiousness.
- Mary is recognized as choosing the better position.

Discovering

The introduction to this account begins with "On their journey..." (10:38). Placing emphasis on *their* reminds us that we are all on the journey with Jesus to God. In this account Martha and Mary are also on the journey with Jesus to God as followers (disciples). Part of discipleship is hospitality, a feature found in the Good Samaritan story. As in that story, Luke presents a question from another perspective. Martha asks, "Lord, are you not concerned that my sister has left me to do the household tasks all alone?" (10:40b). Her point of reference is more on her sister's actions than her own. Mary is not inhospitable since she has chosen the better portion (10:41). Martha, who is anxious and upset, appears to forget true hospitality. Her concern is not on serving but on worrying about how others are serving. True serving is understanding "the one thing that is required" (10:42), that is, to be attentive to Christ and to listen to his word.

Looking Back

On Journey 7 you made the following discoveries:

- Jesus sometimes answers questions by telling a story.
- Jesus' use of a Samaritan in his story gets to the heart of the problem between Jews and Samaritans.
- A complete profile of discipleship includes the concepts of neighbor and hospitality.
- Jesus instructs us on the true meaning of being a neighbor.
- Jesus informs us of the true meaning of hospitality in the account on Martha and Mary.

For Further Exploration

The New Jerome Biblical Commentary, rev. ed., eds. Brown, Raymond E., Joseph Fitzmyer, Roland Murphy. Englewood Cliffs, N.J.: Prentice Hall, 1990.

Perkins, Pheme. *Love Commands in the New Testament*. Ramsey, N.Y.: Paulist Press, 1982.

Journey 8
Reflections on Your Journey

Journey 5 introduced reflective exercises. Here in Journey 8 you again reflect on Luke's faith teachings in order to discover the true meaning of your own journey. This reflective exercise encourages you to place yourself within the Gospel story and create an environment to speak with Jesus in an open and trusting fashion.

Within this Journey, you will incorporate what you have learned from previous exercises. Thus, we can continue with the aim of our study to combine learning in both the head and the heart. The story of Zacchaeus will introduce you to a reflective technique that applies to any scriptural scene in the Gospel.

Read through the entire exercise in order to become comfortable with the steps presented. Then, after the initial reading, do the reflective exercise.

Discovery

- Find a place free of noise and distraction. You will need at least forty minutes to perform this exercise.
- Sit in a chair with your feet flat on the floor, your hands in your lap, your back straight, your eyes lowered or closed.
- Place your Bible on your lap and open it to Luke 19:1-10, the story of Zacchaeus, the tax collector. While reading, try to remember as much of the story's detail as possible. Also, keep a pencil or pen nearby.
- Relax your body by concentrating on your breathing. In the beginning moments of inhaling and exhaling, imagine the following: (1) inhale light, peace, relaxation; (2) exhale fear, anxiety, darkness. Attempt to establish a slow, steady rhythm of inhaling and exhaling.
- Read the biblical passage slowly.
- After reading the story of Zacchaeus, imagine yourself as an onlooker at this biblical scene. Place yourself in the scene by putting yourself in the crowd or near a tree; that is, be a part of the location. Do not hover over the scene or become an outside observer.
- Use your senses to visualize the scene: See the town, the townsfolk, Zacchaeus, the sycamore tree, Jesus. Hear the conversations of all the characters. Smell the aroma of the city. Feel the push of the crowd.
- Notice Zacchaeus climbing the tree. Study his appearance.
- Hear the sounds of the crowd as Jesus passes through it. Spend some time looking at Jesus.
- Hear Jesus tell Zacchaeus he plans to visit his house that day. Use all your senses to notice Zacchaeus's reaction of delight and the crowd's disapproving murmur.
- See and hear Zacchaeus defend himself.
- Hear Jesus tell Zacchaeus salvation has come to his house.
- Slowly begin eliminating details from the scene. Remove all other characters until there are only Jesus, Zacchaeus and you.
- Remove Zacchaeus from the scene so that there are only Jesus and you.
- Spending as much time as needed and in a manner most comfortable to you, speak to Jesus.
- When your conversation has ended, say good-bye to Jesus in a manner comfortable for you.
- When you are ready, open your eyes and begin writing any ideas that come to you. Feel free to express your feelings in prose, poetry or drawings. Let the words or pictures flow onto the paper without forcing any particular ideas. Permit time for pauses during the writing, allowing all ideas to be gathered on paper. Use the space provided below for your written reflection.
- If you are participating in a small group, share your reflection. If you feel comfortable enough in the small group, read all of your writing, summarize the writing or, if the writing is too personal, inform the members you wish to "pass."

Looking Back

On Journey 8 you made the following discoveries:

Journey 9

The Our Father

In previous Journeys we discovered the connection between prayer, the Holy Spirit and action. This Journey focuses on the disciple's need for prayer through a study of the Lord's Prayer.

Discovering

The passage on the Lord's Prayer (Luke 11:1-13) follows the two accounts of the Good Samaritan (10:25ff) and the story of Martha and Mary (10:38ff).

Luke purposefully places the prayer here as part of his careful design for the overall message of his Gospel. In Journey 7 we discovered that Martha neglects a clear understanding of the one thing required (10:42). We also discovered that the entire section is a response to the lawyer's question of "...what must I do to inherit everlasting life?" (10:25). By following these stories with a teaching on prayer, Luke connects the entire section by demonstrating how prayer is essential to gaining everlasting life.

Discovering

Luke is concerned with two issues of his time: (1) how to combat negative influences from outside the community and (2) how to combat negative influences within the community. The outside influences often come from Satan's need to tempt. During Luke's time, the fear of persecution and suffering are causing some members to waiver in their faith. Indeed, the more serious situation is the internal insecurity of the community. Luke may place the question of everlasting life on a lawyer's lips, but it is possible he is asking the same question of his community. Perhaps, like Martha, they have forgotten the one thing required. In seeking a response from his community, Luke is seeking a response from all believers as to what must be done to gain everlasting life.

Discovering

The noted biblical scholar, Eugene LaVerdiere, provides a simple technique for working with a scriptural passage to discover the possible community problem(s) that existed at the time. He encourages students to approach the passage by answering five basic questions: who, what, when, where and why. Responding to these basic questions may provide insight into the community's problems. More importantly, the responses help us discern the heart of the message and the richness of the biblical account.

Read Luke 11:1-13.
Reread Luke 11:1-2.

In the space provided answer who, what, when, where and why. When answering the questions, center on the *person* with the problem, *what* the problem is, *why* there is a problem. Remember there is a variety of responses.

Who has a problem?

What is the problem?

When does the problem occur? (Time)

Where is the problem? (Setting)

Why is there a problem?

Exploring

Let us compare responses to these basic questions.
Who: one of the disciples.
What: The disciples do not know how to pray.
When: "One day..." (11:1). This can be interpreted as any day or every day.
Where: "...in a certain place" (11:1). This can be interpreted as any place.
Why: The disciples want to be true disciples just as John's disciples were.

Discovering

Using your responses from these five questions, write one sentence summarizing the community's problem.

Exploring

To summarize, the disciples are seeking to be people of prayer in order to be true disciples of the Lord.

Discovering

Another technique used to discover the problem is to list the sequence of events in the biblical passage.

Reread Luke 11:1-2. List below the sequence of events.

Exploring

In my rereading of Luke 11:1-2, I discovered the following sequence of events.

- One day the Lord was praying in a certain place.
- After he is finished with prayer, one of the disciples asks him to teach them to pray.
- The disciple addresses him as Lord.
- The Lord teaches them by saying a prayer.

Discovering

Jot down ideas and insights you gained by using these two techniques, asking the basic questions and listing the sequence of events. While reflecting, continue to ask the question: What does all of this mean? (Example: What does it mean that one day Jesus was praying in a certain place?)

Exploring

Here are my insights and ideas gained from my reflection.

The disciple in seeking a solution to his problem asks the Lord to teach him to pray. He seeks an answer only after observing the Lord in prayer. Hence, the disciple views the Lord's praying with awe and respect since he does not pose his question until the prayer time is completed. The individual portrayed as a disciple is representative of all disciples. Even Jesus' response to the man is written as: "He said to 'them' ..." (11:2). As disciples, we recall Luke's emphasis on Jesus as a man of prayer. Refer to the following passages: 5:16; 6:12; 9:18; 10:21-22.

Working with the questions of time (when) and place (where) reveals prayer is essential to all time and can be conducted in any place. Simply, prayer is for every day. Even before providing the *words* of prayer, the Lord is teaching the disciples *how* to pray. Being a good teacher, the Lord teaches by example.

The disciple's addressing him as "Lord" is crucial to the account. It is not Jesus who is addressed here, which would suggest the historical character who lives in a particular time and place. Remember that the Gospel accounts are not biographical sketches of Jesus' life. Rather, the Gospel is a faith account of the Christ which is shared with believers to demonstrate Jesus is the Lord. The time, place, setting and words are more than historical data and should be examined for their revelation about God through the risen Lord. Hence, the title, *Lord*, is addressed to the risen Savior who is beyond time and place and who has conquered sin and death. The one who is teaching prayer is the Lord, the Resurrected One.

The answer to the *why* of prayer conveys the disciple's wish to be a true disciple. If the Lord prays, then his disciples must pray. Yet, this prayer is different from the prayer of John since John the Baptizer is not the Lord. On a deeper level, the *why* of prayer is continually being unfolded by Luke who associates prayer with the coming of the Holy Spirit. The Spirit comes at prayer and prepares the disciple for ministry.

Discovery

Read Luke 11:3-4.

The words of the Lord's Prayer can be divided into two main sections: the awareness of God as Father and the petitions requested in prayer.

The first section does not originate with Jesus. The Israelites came to recognize God as their Father.

Read Sirach 23:1-4.

Although not originated by Jesus, this reference to God as Father does suggest a deep relationship between the Father and Jesus. Luke makes reference to this relationship in previous passages. We need to examine these references as background to understand the relationship between Jesus and the Father.

Discovering

Read Luke 3:21-22.

In this account the Father refers to Jesus as his beloved Son. It is his beloved Son now filled with the Spirit on whom the Father's favor rests.

Discovering

We must reflect on the meaning of the word *father* to complete our study of God as Father. This reflection cannot be focused on our own biological fathers but rather on the term itself without attachment to specific individuals. This calls for a *transformation of consciousness*, which is a change of view. Instead of looking at *father* to determine what it means, the transformation of consciousness requires viewing from the father's perspective. In other words, what does it mean for one to *be* a father?

Using the transformation of consciousness, list below three to five qualities of fatherhood.

Exploring

I have listed the following qualities of fatherhood:

- Father implies a relationship.
- Father is linked with procreation.
- Father is seen as a protector.
- Father is a provider.
- Father is loving.

Discovering

Read Luke 11:11.

Luke provides a transformation of consciousness by relating a point from a father's perspective. In a sense, Luke is asking: As a father how should I respond to my children's needs? His reply: A father responds by being one who will give what is requested.

The Lord, in addressing God as Father, understands the transformation of consciousness. He invites all disciples to address God as Father, which unites the disciple with God and Christ. Through this union, the disciple realizes that all people have God as Father; therefore, all people are brother and sister to each other.

Discovering

"Hallowed be your name..." (11:2) immediately follows the address to God as *Father*. Although God's name is holy (hallowed), it is not given. The Old Testament reveals God's name as "I am who am" (Exodus 3:14). However, the Old Testament writers, out of a sense of awe for God, refuse to use the name of God and begin referring to God by title, i.e., Lord. They realize to truly know God, demonstrated by knowing God's name, is beyond human capability. All they knew was that God is the ultimate holy, and God's name is hallowed.

Discovering

The second section of the Lord's Prayer is four petitions. The first petition is for the coming of the Kingdom of God. This is Christ's mission: to bring about the Kingdom, which is the redemptive presence of God. Luke has Jesus making this announcement when he claims, "Go and report to John what you have seen and heard. The blind recover their sight, cripples walk, lepers are cured, the deaf hear, dead men are raised to life, and the poor have the good news preached to them" (Luke 7:22). Jesus, instructing the disciples to ask this petition in prayer, is teaching them to be ministers of bringing about the Kingdom of God.

Discovering

The second petition, asking for "daily bread," involves a meal. Bread is the basic staple for nourishment. The disciple is being taught to ask for the daily supplement—all the things needed both physically and spiritually in order to continue to do the work of the Father. The first petition has already informed us that that work of the Father concerns the kingdom.

Discovering

We have discovered in previous Journeys that Peter's response to the call from Christ was the admission of his sinfulness. The need for forgiveness then is the first need of any disciple. Just as the Father forgives the disciple in response to this petition, the disciple in turn models this action and forgives all others.

Discovering

The final petition is a realization that the journey to God is a journey to truth. Just as Christ was tempted to turn from the truth, the disciple also will be tempted. The final request asks God's assistance in resisting evil.

Discovery

Read Luke 11:5-13.

Luke concludes the lesson on prayer with the command to be persistent. This persistence will "...give him [us] as much as he [we] needs" (11:8). The giving is not what we *think* we need, but what we truly need to lead a Christian life on the journey to God. This giving comes through the Holy Spirit (11:13b). Here Luke again repeats the theme of prayer leading to the Spirit's coming for ministry.

We can conclude from our study that the praying of the Lord's Prayer is a prayer for discipleship. As disciples, we pray to the Father through the Spirit to live out daily the call of the Christian life.

Looking Back

On Journey 9 you made the following discoveries:

- Prayer is essential to gaining everlasting life.
- Reflecting on the five basic questions and their responses provides insight into the problems experienced by the community.
- The Our Father is the prayer of the Lord.
- Reference to God as *Father* emphasizes the familial relationship among all people.
- Prayer is associated with the Holy Spirit coming to prepare the disciple for ministry.
- The Our Father prayer consists of two parts: an address to God as Father and petitions.
- Not only are disciples encouraged to pray, but they are to be persistent in their prayer.

For Further Exploration

LaVerdiere, Eugene. *When We Pray: Meditations on the Lord's Prayer.* Notre Dame, Ind.: Ave Maria Press, 1983.

Merton, Thomas. *Our Father: Perfect Prayer*, Audiocassette. Kansas City, Mo.: Credence Cassettes, 1989.

Journey 10
Praying the Our Father

Journey 9 introduced the Lord's Prayer as the prayer of a disciple. As the Lord's disciples, we seek ways to continue our relationship with God through prayer. Although there are many styles of praying, one technique called centering prayer seems appropriate because it uses the Our Father.

Discovering

Centering prayer is a method of finding God within oneself. It encourages the participant to place aside all distractions and bask in the loving presence of God. It encourages the person to heed the psalmist suggestion to "Desist! and confess that I am God" (Psalm 46:11). The suggestions for practicing centering prayer are fairly simple. Read the entire exercise first and then follow each step.

- Find a quiet place free from distractions. You will need twenty minutes for this exercise. Plan some way to mark the end of the time without having to look at your watch or clock. A silent cassette tape with a slight sound at the end of twenty minutes may be appropriate.
- Place yourself in a relaxed position. Often it is helpful to concentrate on your breathing. As you inhale, imagine the peace and love of God entering your body. As you exhale, imagine anxiety and frustration leaving your body.
- Select one word that expresses the loving presence of God for you, for example, *Father, Lord, Christ, Lover.* Repeat this word slowly and reverently until it becomes one with your breathing.
- Whenever something distracts you (a noise, a thought) return gently to your one holy word. Place the distraction on an imaginary shelf or in an imaginary garbage bag.
- At the end of twenty minutes, begin praying the Our Father slowly and quietly.

Those who practice centering prayer recommend two prayer periods each day: morning and evening.

Looking Back

On Journey 10 you made the following discovery:

- The technique for practicing centering prayer.

For Further Exploration

Anonymous. *The Cloud of Unknowing.* Middlesex, England: Penguin Books Ltd., 1961.

Pennington, Basil. *Daily We Touch Him: Practical Religious Experiences.* Garden City, N.Y.: Doubleday and Company, 1977.

Journey 11

Lost + Found = Joy

When I was a young boy, my mother had very few rules for me to follow. One major household law, however, was to stay clear of the contents in my mother's purse. Whenever I wanted to "borrow" something, the first condition was to bring her the pocketbook.

One summer day, when I was nine, my mother accused me of going to her purse and taking ten dollars without her permission. Despite my denials, she insisted that since the money was gone, and I was the only person in the house, I had to be the culprit. Punishment from my mother was the disappointing tone in her voice as she kept drilling me for the money. Even though I did not take the money, I began feeling guilty. She ceased her interrogation and allowed me to continue to play outside with my friends. For some reason, this release did not ease my guilt.

One hour had passed when my mother called for me again. Believing I was in for more questioning, I reluctantly entered the house. To my surprise, my mother was waving the ten dollar bill in her hand. Realizing she had placed the money in another location, she began apologizing for her accusation. At that point, she placed the ten dollars in my hand and explained that since she thought it was lost, I should have the money. I was overjoyed and for the remainder of that summer hoped and prayed my mother would misplace some more money!

Discovering

I always remember the story of my mother and the ten dollars when reading Luke 15. Just as there was great joy in my household on that special summer day over finding the lost money, Luke provides similar stories with themes of joy over finding something or someone lost.

Read Luke 15.

In the space provided list the events and stories in this chapter.

Exploring

Compare your list with mine.

- The Pharisees and scribes accuse Jesus of eating with tax collectors and sinners.
- Jesus tells the story of the shepherd who finds his lost sheep and celebrates.
- Jesus tells the story of the woman who finds a lost coin and celebrates.
- Jesus tells the story of a father who, upon the return of his lost son, celebrates.

Discovering

Reread Luke 15:1-2.

Answer the following questions:

1) Who has the problem?

2) What is the problem?

Exploring

The scribes and Pharisees have a problem with Jesus eating with sinners. Jesus, the tax collectors and sinners, however, have no problem being with each other.

Discovering

We reviewed a similar situation in the Good Samaritan story (Luke 10:25ff) where the lawyer is unable to mention the name, *Samaritan*. Luke is always introducing two categories of people: outsiders and insiders. But Luke also asks for a transformation of consciousness (a change in view) which determines who is truly an outsider or insider.

From a legalistic viewpoint, the tax collectors and sinners are outsiders because they are unclean and excluded from the Temple. For the most part, the Pharisees and scribes, as men of the law and external observers of that law, are insiders. From a gospel perspective and by leading a life of love, however, Jesus associates with tax collectors and sinners thus making the tax collectors and sinners insiders. In this case, the Pharisees and scribes who misuse the law are the outsiders.

Discovering

Background to this juxtaposition of insiders and outsiders is found in Luke 14.

Read Luke 14:1-35.

In the following exercise divide the space provided below into two columns. Entitle one column "Insiders" and the other "Outsiders." Under the appropriate column, write a phrase naming the character and the action that determines a person as an insider or outsider. In making your list, read the above passage from a legalistic point of view (i.e., read the passage with a strict, literal view of conformity to religious code).

Exploring

Compare your listing with mine:

Insiders

- Pharisees who are silent when questioned by Jesus (14:4a)
- Pharisees who cannot answer
- the arrogant guest
- hosts who invite friends to a dinner party (14:12b)
- people who make excuses
- people who cannot renounce possessions or family

Outsiders

- man with dropsy
- Jesus
- the humble guest
- hosts who invite strangers (14:13)
- the poor and crippled
- people who take up their cross and renounce all

Notice how the list of outsiders is similar to the characters referred to in Luke 7:18ff, a Gospel section entitled "Jesus' Testimony."

Discovery

In his welcoming of sinners to the table, a gesture one does with friends (insiders), Jesus demonstrates the meaning of hospitality and community. These themes of table ministry, hospitality and community will be discussed in other Journeys.

Reread Luke 15:3-10.

In the space provided below list any writing techniques you found in this passage. Write a short paragraph summarizing the revelations about faith and God from the two stories (the lost sheep and the lost coin).

Exploring

Again Luke introduces a balance between his stories: (a) man and woman: the story involving a man (shepherd) is followed by a story about a woman (lost coin), and (b) lost and found: there is great joy over something (someone) who is lost. This joy is the joy of God who is like the shepherd who found his sheep and the woman who found her coin.

Discovery

After rereading specific verses of the Prodigal Son story, comment on the meaning *behind* the information given rather than the literal picture presented. While searching for each verse's meaning, assume you do not know the rest of the story.

Read Luke 15:11.
Write:

Read Luke 15:12.
Write:

Read Luke 15:13-16.
Write:

Read Luke 15:17-20.
Write:

Read Luke 15:21-24.
Write:

Read Luke 15:25-28.
Write:

Read Luke 15:29-32.
Write:

Exploration

The following are my comments on these verses. Do not be concerned if they are not exactly the same as yours. Our purpose is to have a listing for reflection and discussion.

- *Luke 15:11.* We are introduced to a family of two sons and one father. *Family* assumes relationship and harmony between the members. The story begins with this harmony.
- *Luke 15:12.* The younger son wishes to break from the family thus causing a disharmony. The backdrop to this passage is found in the Old Testament.

    Read Genesis 4:1-16.

    In this account Cain murders his brother Abel. The consequence of his sin is to be a restless wanderer (4:12). Cain will have no roots, no meaning and no purpose to his life. He becomes separated from all other life. The story does not end here, however. God gives Cain a tribal mark which does not allow others to kill him at sight (4:15).

This mark by God is a sign of forgiveness claiming that Cain belongs.

- *Luke 15:13-16.* The consequences of the younger son's actions are despicable. Not only has he disassociated himself from his family, but by eating the fodder of pigs, he disassociates himself from the whole Jewish tradition. (Read Leviticus 11:7-8 for background on the Jewish rule of abstaining from pork.)
- *Luke 15:17-21.* The son comes to his senses and seeks forgiveness.
- *Luke 15:22-24.* The father welcomes the son home and reestablishes the harmony that was lost. The son becomes a part of the family signified by the clothing and ring given by the father. In celebration, a banquet is prepared.
- *Luke 15:25-28.* The older son, in his resentment toward his father and brother, refuses to enter the banquet. He causes disharmony and breaks the relationship of the family.
- *Luke 15:29-32.* These verses point to the difficulty some of the faithful (older brother) have accepting the repentant sinner. Notice the older brother's comment, "this son" (15:30), which suggests his inability to accept his brother. The father reminds him, however, of the family relationship with the words, "this brother of yours..." (15:32). The loving father acts like God by rejoicing over the return of his son.

Discovering

We exit the story without ever knowing whether the older brother enters the banquet. This may be deliberate on Luke's part so that he may ask what we would do in this situation:

If I were the older brother, would I enter the banquet?

If yes, what would be my behavior once inside the party?

If no, what would be my motive for not attending the party?

Am I able to forgive the lost and see them again as part of my family?

Do I desire chaos? or harmony?

Looking Back

On Journey 11 you made the following discoveries:

- the idea of "insiders" and "outsiders" from both the Gospel and the legalistic perspectives;
- the reason behind Jesus' association with sinners and tax collectors;
- the joy of God when finding someone lost;
- the harmony required within the Christian community.

For Further Exploration

LaVerdiere, Eugene. *The Gospel of Luke*, Audiocassettes. Austin, Texas: Texas Catholic Conference Scripture Seminar, October 28-31, 1985.

Perkins, Pheme. *Reading the New Testament*, 2nd ed. Mahwah, N.J.: Paulist Press, 1988.

Journey 12

If You Want Peace—Work for Justice (Paul VI)

Mary Reed Newland, who spent her life as a catechist and storyteller, defined justice as "the way God is." Her definition captures the heart of all of the Scriptures in general and the Lucan Gospel specifically. In the announcement of the Kingdom of God, Jesus proclaims the redemptive presence of God for all people. By referring to God as Father, Jesus suggests a relationship in which all people are brothers and sisters. It is not God who creates situations of racism, alienation, greed and hate, but humans. In terms of Luke's Gospel, it is not God who created insiders and outsiders, but most of the Pharisees, scribes and some townsfolk.

Discovering

Read Luke 8:26-38.
  In the space provided answer the following questions.

Who has the problem?

What is the problem?

Exploring

The initial response in determining the problem may center on the Gerasene demoniac with his possession of evil spirits which are legion (many). The demoniac's problem, however, is healed by the power of Jesus who is recognized as the Son of God Most High. Closer examination draws attention to the townsfolk who, on seeing the cured man, are terrified (8:35). Uncomfortable with the change in the demoniac and the ability of Jesus to bring about this change, they ask Jesus to leave their neighborhood (8:37).

Discovering

Working toward justice often requires change, a change that has certain characteristics. Justice aims at discovering the core of the problem and bringing about a systemic change. The procedures to bring about change are often considered extremely controversial. In the passage on the demoniac, the people are comfortable with the bizarre behavior of the man as long as he was possessed. Now that he is whole, a condition meant for all, the townsfolk are uncomfortable and view Jesus' action as controversial. By banishing Jesus, they hope to banish any other changes that have to be made. The townsfolk realize that change is difficult, especially change that forces a perspective on how God sees things or "the way God is!"

Discovering

Jesus' distaste for injustice is highlighted numerous times in Luke.
  Read Luke 11:37-52.

Exploring

Here we read of Jesus' chastisement of the Pharisees and lawyers of the day. They spend more time on external values than the internal values of justice and the love of God (11:42).

Discovering

Luke presents a contrast between the values taught about the Kingdom by Jesus and the values upheld by the majority of Pharisees, lawyers and scribes of the time. These anti-Kingdom values are no different than the values upheld by today's society.
  Read Luke 17.
  Under each column, list the value taught by Jesus in contrast to the opposing value taught by today's society.

Kingdom Values (Luke 17)

Society's Values

Write a paragraph of what this passage is either saying about the way of the Kingdom or the way of the world.

Exploring

Together our listings will provide further insight into our study of justice.

Kingdom Values
    Avoid scandal.
    Forgiveness
    Inner personal faith
    Be a servant.
    Gratitude
    Be on guard.
    Live in the presence of God daily.

Society's Values
    Do what you want, don't get caught; if you do get caught,
        have enough power and money to get out of it.
    Revenge
    Self-righteousness
    Take all you can.
    Greed
    If it feels good, do it.
    Remember God and faith only in times of crisis.

Discovering

Luke continues to provide stories that contrast these two sets of values. He challenges us to find in his stories either ways of the Kingdom or ways of the world. This challenge has recently been accepted by laypeople who, while working with Luke's theme of justice, have provided new insight into particular passages. I was first introduced to these new ideas by Franciscan priest Richard Rohr during a weekend retreat at St. Thomas University. According to Father Rohr, biblical discussions among the economically poor of Central and South America have forced biblical scholars to view certain accounts in a new light.
    Read Luke 19:11-27.

Exploring

For years, my approach to this passage said something of the way of the Kingdom. At some time, I will be accountable to the talents given me by God. I cannot bury these talents but must use them and share them with others.
    With the new insights offered to me by Richard Rohr, my understanding of this passage has changed dramatically. Viewed as an account of the way of the world, the passage affirms oppression and greed: a situation in opposition to the values of God's Kingdom. The passage has little or nothing to say about the talents given to me by God.

Discovering

It is helpful when studying Scripture to learn all one can about the historical situation at the time the passage was written. This study is sometimes referred to as a study of *that history*. A primary source for background into *that history* are the writings of Josephus, a first-century Jewish historian (37-100 B.C.E.). Josephus makes reference to Archelaus, who sought to be king. While seeking recognition in Rome for more than three years, Archelaus placed people in charge of his home territory. They were to continue in the manner of Archelaus, which was to overtax the people. Upon his return, Archelaus rewarded those delegates who maintained the territory in an unjust manner. With this historical background, some people claim the reference to "a man of noble birth..." is Archelaus. His travel to a faraway country to become its king is Archelaus's journey to Rome.

The historical information helps us understand the fundamental purpose or moral of the biblical account. In Luke 19:26 the action of the king may reflect the ways of the world, but it does not reflect the ways of God's Kingdom. In the entire chapter of Luke 19, the contrast between the two kingdoms is presented. Zacchaeus gaining salvation (19:1-10) is representative of the Kingdom of God, while the systems of Archelaus represent the unjust world (19:11-27).

Discovering

The contrast between the two kingdoms is best summarized in another parable of Jesus.
Read Luke 18:9-14.

Exploring

Notice Luke's use of irony in his portrayal of the Pharisee. He paints this picture of the Pharisee in contrast to another image presented in Luke 11 where the Pharisee is accused of being hypocritical and unjust. In Luke 18 the Pharisee prays as a person who "fast(s) twice a week...and tithes on all possess(ed)," similar to what a *just* man does.

The real image of the Pharisee is in contrast with the image of the tax collector. The tax collector is reminiscent of Peter, who, on being called by God, realizes his sinfulness. Because of his realization, Jesus sees him as the *true* just man. Finally, the contrasts demonstrated in these two characters exemplify another key teaching by Jesus; that is, to be humble and willing to serve.

Discovery

There are consequences to acting justly. In the discussion of Luke 6, Jesus instructs us that announcing the Kingdom will have men hating, ostracizing and insulting us. Luke 11 concludes with the Pharisees' beginning to manifest fierce hostility and setting traps to catch Jesus (11:53-54). Although our study has not yet taken us to the crucifixion, we know the results of Jesus' ministry. He will be hated, ostracized, insulted and finally persecuted and killed. Jesus' life of working for justice will lead to his passion and death.

Exploring

This lesson on justice and its consequences has been a part of our history. More recently throughout the world, we have witnessed women and men persecuted because of their stand for justice. I mention only a few by name for purposes of quiet reflection:
  Mohandas Gandhi
  Martin Luther King, Jr.
  Oscar Romero
  Jean Donovan
  Ita Ford
  Maura Clarke
  Dorothy Kazel
  Ignacio Ellacuria
  Joaquin Lopez y Lopez
  Amando Lopez
  Ignacio Martin-Baro
  Segundo Montes
  Juan Ramon Moreno
  Celina Ramos
  Julia Elba Ramos
  and hundreds and thousands more....

Looking Back

On Journey 12 you made the following discoveries:

- Justice is the way God is.
- Justice works toward systemic change and is often considered controversial.
- Jesus accuses the Pharisees and lawyers of being unjust people.
- Luke's Gospel presents a contrast between values of the Kingdom of God and values of society.
- A life working for justice may lead to persecution and death.

For Further Exploration

Karris, Robert J. *Luke: Artist and Theologian*. Mahwah, N.J.: Paulist Press, 1985.

Rohr, Richard. *Working for Justice*, Video program. Miami, Fla.: St. Thomas University Media Center, January 1990.

Journey 13

Meals and the Messianic Banquet

Meals play an important role in our lives. Besides being necessary for survival, they gather together relatives and friends. Most, if not all, of our celebrations center around a meal. Jesus, in Luke's Gospel, is often depicted as a picnic-goer ready to share a meal with others. This meal activity of Jesus permeates almost every chapter of Luke's Gospel, and has been hinted at in our Journeys about Martha, the Prodigal Son and Zacchaeus.

Discovering

We need to view the sharing of a meal as a sign that points to another reality. In biblical understanding, the sharing of a meal signifies the reality that one does not sit at table with enemies but with friends. Jesus' willingness to sit at table with a variety of peoples, especially tax collectors and sinners, becomes a sign of this new reality. By doing this, Jesus points to the coming of the Messianic banquet and the announcement of the Kingdom of God. At this banquet with God, brought on by the Messiah, all the saved will sit together for ever and ever.

Discovering

Luke presented this new reality in the beginning of his Gospel. Remember our study of the birth of Jesus and the emphasis on "...and laid him in a manger" (Luke 2:7). Christ, in the manger, becomes the food for humanity which allows angels to sing and shepherds to come and see. From the infancy narratives to the post-Resurrection accounts, the meal theme is central to Luke's presentation of Jesus. Indeed, the biblical scholar, Robert Karris, counts more than forty-five different words referring to food in Luke's Gospel.

Discovering

The Old Testament is another resource for background information to the meal theme in Luke. Many scholars uphold that the core of the Old Testament message is found in the Exodus/Sinai story. Here the Israelites are freed from slavery and brought through the sea of death to a journey toward the promised land and new life. Crucial to understanding this saga are numerous biblical symbols, one of which is the Passover meal.

Skim Exodus 12—20.

The entire historical event of moving from slavery to freedom becomes the origin for a liturgical celebration. In Exodus 12, the food, its preparation and the instructions on how it is to be eaten are presented as ritual rather than mere data. This is comparable to our Thanksgiving feast in which special foods are essential to celebrating the day. There is nothing thankful in a turkey, yet the turkey meal becomes a national ritual as a sign of our dependence upon God.

In the Exodus/Sinai account, the meal celebration signifies the sealing of the covenant given by God to Moses (Exodus 20). We ordinarily refer to this covenant as the Ten Commandments. From the Israelites' viewpoint, these commandments are signposts for living a life with God. Realizing that God gives life, the Israelites eat a meal in which certain elements of the meal signify this new life with God.

Discovering

Within the Passover meal, three elements become signs.

1) The ritual of the sacrifice of the lamb and the painting of the doorpost with lamb's blood allows the angel of death to pass over (*pesach*) the homes of the Israelites.

Scholars differ over the etymology of *pesach*. It may come from an Akkadian root (*pasahu*) meaning "to appease" or "to limp or leap." The latter connection of "leaping" comes from a sacred dance of leaping around a sacred object. The "appeasement" may come from an existing Akkadian ritual. Some scholars suggest that the word *pesach* is rooted in an Egyptian translation meaning "to strike a blow." Despite the difference of opinion over the etymology of the word, the event celebrates the night in which Yahweh passed over the houses and spared the lives of the firstborn.

2) The next sign is the unleavened bread (*massoth*). Canaanite housewives used a piece of old dough in each new day's batch of bread. At the time of the spring massoth, they cleaned the house, removed the old dough and started a new dough which was unleavened. Borrowed from a Canaanite harvest festival, the eating of unleavened bread becomes a sign of new beginnings. This new beginning for the Israelites is their movement from slavery under Pharaoh to new life in the promised land.

3) The third sign is the consecration of the firstborn (*qadesh*). This practice acknowledges that God (Yahweh) has dominion over all creation. God does not

want child sacrifice (a practice of the Ammorites) but redemption. This consecration of the firstborn commemorates the idea that God brought the Israelites out of slavery.

Discovering

Read Luke 9:10-17.
What connection can be made between the Exodus/Sinai event and this miracle of Jesus? (Reread Exodus 16.)

Exploring

The connection I make between the two readings centers on the desert of Exodus 16 with the "...out-of-the-way place" mentioned in Luke 9:12. Just as in the desert God feeds the Israelites, so now Christ feeds the people. In both accounts humanity is fed by God because of the special relationship God has with the people. Being fed by either God in the desert or Christ in Bethsaida says something about the relationship between people: They are now kin. Remember one does not sit down and eat with enemies but with relatives and friends.

Discovering

Further investigation into Luke 9:16 reveals a ritual action on the part of Jesus. He takes the loaves, raises his eyes, pronounces a blessing, breaks the bread and gives it to his disciples to distribute to the people.

This ritual action reminds us of the daily bread we ask for in the recitation of the Our Father. In that prayer we ask God to give us all that we need to perform the actions necessary to bring about the Kingdom of God. We view the prayer as a prayer of discipleship. In the multiplication of the loaves the disciples' distribution of the bread symbolizes their being instructed by Christ and doing for others what the Lord has done for them.

Discovering

Read Luke 22:7-20.
What connections do you make between Luke 22:7-20

and the Exodus/Sinai event or the account in Luke 9:10-17?

Exploring

I have made the following connections:

• The day of Unleavened Bread, when the paschal lamb is slain, unites this story with the Passover event of Exodus 12.
• The Passover preparation begins the Passion story of Jesus. Just as the Passover meal is connected with the Mosaic covenant, this Lord's meal is connected to a new covenant established by Jesus' passion, death and resurrection.
• Jesus' ritual actions of taking the cup and the bread during the Last Supper are similar to the ritual described in Luke 9.

Discovering

This last connection between the ritual of the Last Supper and the ritual of the multiplication of loaves suggests Jesus performed this rite many times. It is possible that Jesus often took bread, blessed it and distributed it. This Last Supper account epitomizes all of the previous bread-blessing performed by Jesus and becomes the ultimate example of Christ's action in instituting the Eucharist. The image presented of the disciples at table with the Lord points to a eucharistic image of all humanity sitting at table with God. When we come together and eat and drink at Eucharist we profess our union with Christ and our community with one another.

Discovering

Read Luke 22:21.
Note that *The New American Bible* subheading, The Betrayer, follows the account of the Holy Eucharist. The results of Jesus' sitting at table with his disciples will lead one of his disciples to betray him. We can also say it was all of Jesus' actions of eating and drinking with the alienated and the poor which lead to his death.

Looking Back

On Journey 13 you made these discoveries:

- In Scripture, when people share a meal, this action points to a new reality of friendship.
- There are connections between the meals of Jesus and the Passover meal of the Old Testament.
- Some of the meals in Scripture have deep liturgical significance.
- The Last Supper meal epitomizes all of the eucharistic-type meals celebrated by Jesus.
- The manner in which Jesus shared a meal with people may be another reason for his passion and death.

For Further Exploration

Boadt, Lawrence. *Reading the Old Testament: An Introduction*. Mahwah, N.J.: Paulist Press, 1984.

Karris, Robert. *Luke: Artist and Theologian*. Mahwah, N.J.: Paulist Press, 1985.

LaVerdiere, Eugene. "Do This In Memory of Me," Parts I and II, *The Gospel of Luke*, Audiocassettes. Austin, Texas: Texas Catholic Conference Scripture Seminar, 1985.

Journey 14

Reflecting on the Journey to Jerusalem

The journey to God with Jesus culminates in Jerusalem. An essential part of the journey is the passion and death of Jesus. Luke provides a more detailed account of the passion and death than the other Gospel writers. His intention is to invite the reader to follow along with Jesus and experience the Passion with him. The purpose of this Journey is to reflect on this dramatic moment in Jesus' life as a preparation to a more critical analysis in Journey 15.

The techniques for following Jesus in Jerusalem are similar to techniques for reflective reading you learned in previous Journeys:

- Find a place where you can be alone to read and reflect quietly. You may need one hour for this exercise.
- Open your Bible to Luke 22:39 and leave the Bible open for easy access.
- Begin to relax your body. Starting with the soles of your feet and gently moving up each part of your body to the top of your head, imagine the peace of God filling your entire body.
- Whisper slowly, "Thank you, Father, for loving me."
- Begin to imagine that you are a Jew of the first century. See yourself near Jesus and the twelve apostles as they begin sharing the Passover meal. Find a place within the upper room where you can observe and be a part of the scene. Smell the special foods of the seder meal. Taste the unleavened bread and the roasted lamb. Notice the activity within the room.
- At the end of the meal, walk with Jesus and his disciples as they move through the winding streets of Jerusalem. Proceed with them down the Roman steps into the Kidron Valley until you enter the Mount of Olives.
- Begin reading from Luke 22:39. Whisper softly what you read. Do not rush nor read at an artificially slow pace. When something strikes you, stop and ponder the idea. If you tire of reading, pause and reflect until you are ready to move on.
- Discontinue reading when you reach Luke 23:46b, "After he said this, he expired."
- Pause for a moment and imagine a scene of only you looking up at Jesus on the cross. Spend time in private, personal prayer.
- In the space provided answer the following three questions:

What did I see in Jerusalem?

How do I think Jesus is feeling during this time?

How did I feel during and after this meeting with Jesus?

Looking Back

On Journey 14 you made the following discoveries:

Journey 15
Passion, Death, Resurrection

As noted in the previous Journey, Luke provides a more detailed account of Jesus' passion and death than the other Gospel writers. Providing mere details is not Luke's intention, however. Rather, he wants his readers to see the entire Gospel coming to a climax in the passion, death and resurrection. His account is rich in imagery, thus inviting the reader to draw on previous Gospel images and to reflect on current pastoral situations.

Discovering

Inherent to the Christian faith is the realization that there is no resurrection without suffering and, likewise, there is no suffering without the promise of resurrection. Each complements the other and needs to be studied for interconnections. Luke does not want the reader to be so eager to jump to the passage on the tomb without first contemplating the scene at the cross. In every part of the account Luke desires the reader to search for the Passion-Resurrection connection.

Discovering

Luke's Passion-Resurrection account is filled with irony thus creating a tension between characters and ideas. Many times he is working on two levels: the story itself and the message for the contemporary Christian community.

For each account listed, write the connection between the Passion and the Resurrection, the tension between characters or ideas, and the message for the community.

Read Luke 22:3; 22:31; 22:40; 22:46.

Write your responses in the space following each account.

Luke 22:3

Luke 22:31

Luke 22:40

Luke 22:46

Exploring

In these accounts the betrayal of Jesus is under the direction of Satan and will lead to Jesus' death. Yet the irony is that through this death Jesus will conquer the reign of Satan and establish a new reign of the Kingdom of God. The battle with Satan has not ended, however, since it is evil that still "ask(s) for you, to sift you all like wheat" (22:31). Realizing this ongoing cosmic battle of good and evil exists, the community must be aware of Satan's continual testing to lure them from God.

Discovering

Read Luke 22:54-62.

What connection can be made between this account of Peter's denial and the previous work concerning Satan and the trial?

Exploring

Satan tempts Peter in the form of three individuals: a servant girl, a man and the person Peter refers to as "friend." He submits to the temptation and again realizes he is a sinner, thus connecting this scene with Luke 5:8.

But Jesus' look and Peter's seeking of forgiveness helps us realize that Peter will become a great disciple. This is a point that will be affirmed in the Book of Acts. Through Jesus' forgiveness of Peter and Peter's forgiveness of himself, the community is again reminded of the Lucan theme to forgive one another.

Discovering

Read Luke 22:63-64; 22:70; 23:3; 23:35-39.

What irony do you find in each of these accounts?

Exploring

All of the accusations against Jesus of his being a prophet (22:63-64), the Son of God (22:70), king of the Jews (23:3) and the Messiah of God (23:35ff) are actually correct. But Jesus does not claim any of this recognition and often replies, "It is you who say I am" (22:70). These accusations will lead to his Passion and Resurrection, which will proclaim Jesus as the Son of God, King and Messiah.

Discovering

Read Luke 23:26; 23:27-30; 23:34; 23:35; 23:32, 39-43.

What do each of these situations or characters represent to the entire Christian community?

Simon carrying the cross.

The women weeping for Jesus.

The people rolling dice for Jesus' garments.

The jeering crowd asking Jesus to save himself.

The two prisoners crucified alongside Jesus.

Exploring

Simon the Cyrenean represents the person willing to follow Christ. He takes up the cross with Jesus and like Jesus was willing to take up his own cross. This cross is not imposed as some handicap or inability but is freely chosen. All of these points suggest Simon's character serves as another example of discipleship.

The women should not weep for Jesus who is innocent (like "green wood," Luke 23). This statement is a foreshadowing of the razing of Jerusalem and the judgment of those who are guilty. It is also parallel to the sayings of Jesus found in Luke 21:20-24.

Those who roll the dice fulfill the sayings of Psalm 22:19, "they divide my garments among them,/and for my vesture they cast lots."

The jeering crowd asking Jesus to save himself does not realize that it is the Christ who will save us all.

The two criminals represent the difference between those people who look for an immediate earthly reward and those who are looking to gain paradise. This contrast has been prevalent in Luke's Gospel, and reminds us of the story of the Pharisee and the tax collector (Luke 18:9-14).

Discovering

Read Luke 23:46b-56.

What are the reactions to the death of Jesus? What do these reactions say to the contemporary Christian?

What is the reaction of the centurion? What does this reaction mean for us?

What is the reaction of the crowd? What does this reaction mean for us?

What is the reaction of his friends?

What is the reaction of Joseph from Arimathea? What does his reaction say?

Exploring

The centurion, the executor, becomes the believer.
    The people who jeered are repentant.
    The friends witness everything from a distance.
    Joseph of Arimathea is a holy member of the Sanhedrin. The Sanhedrin was part of the assembly responsible for Jesus' death. It now has a member honoring the body with burial.

Discovering: Resurrection

The earliest account of the Resurrection of Jesus is found in Paul's epistles and not the Gospels.
    Read I Corinthians 15:3-8.
    Read Luke 24:1-11.
    Compare Luke's account of the Resurrection with Paul's.
    What differences did you discover between these two accounts?

Exploring

- Luke mentions a time of day (early in the morning) whereas Paul does not.
- Luke mentions women coming to the tomb whereas Paul never mentions women.
- Luke mentions certain happenings and provides dialogue between characters whereas Paul gives the fundamental teaching: Jesus died, was buried and rose.

Discovering

Although we discovered major differences between Paul's and Luke's presentation of the Resurrection, there is one essential similarity between them. Both claim that Jesus died, was buried and rose. Neither of them is speaking of resuscitation where the individual returns from death in the same earthly body. Rather both of them present *resurrection*, which is the *transformation* of the body so that it will never die again. Along with this core truth about Jesus' Resurrection, Paul and Luke include either names, scenes, dialogues or events. Each of these inclusions points in some way to resurrection.

Discovering

Reread Luke 24:1-11.

After reading the Lucan account, answer the following questions.

Using biblical eyes and ears, what connection from Scripture can you make with Luke's time for the Resurrection? See Luke 24:1.

What are some possibilities as to why the body is not in the tomb?

What is the significance of the two men in dazzling garments?

What is your understanding of the men's statement in Luke 24:5-8?

What is the significance of Peter's amazement upon seeing the wrappings in the tomb?

Exploring

The reference to the first day of the week, at dawn, is reminiscent of the creation account of Genesis 1. Just as God began creation with light so we have a new creation occurring with the dawn light of resurrection.

There are several possibilities as to why there is no body in the tomb. The body could have been stolen in order to trick the Roman and Jewish officials. The body was never placed in the tomb originally, and thus was placed in another location. The body is resurrected and left the tomb empty. Of all the possibilities, the last one regarding resurrection requires faith. You cannot historically document or scientifically prove resurrection. You can only believe it. Luke's images of people coming to an empty tomb is saying something about people's faith and their witness to that faith.

The two men in dazzling garments are another example of Luke's concept of discipleship. Throughout all of his Gospel disciples are sent in pairs to preach the Good News. The core of these two men's proclamation is the Good News preached by all disciples: Jesus is risen from the dead—He is Lord!

We have already discovered that the two men are preaching resurrection. Their question of "Why do you search for the Living One among the dead?" (24:5) is a proclamation that resurrection has conquered death and Jesus is true Life. Throughout Jesus' time with the disciples, he predicted the passion, death and resurrection. These occurrences have happened as all of Jesus' predictions have happened. As believers, we do not look for life where there is death (a tomb), but for life where Jesus is. Where he is, is not in the tomb!

Peter's amazement does not suggest that he understands Christ has resurrected from the dead. Rather his amazement signifies his wondering and pondering over what has happened to this Jesus. This is the same type of amazement held by the people in the Temple who were amazed at Jesus' intelligence and his answers (Luke 2:47).

Looking Back

On Journey 15 you made the following discoveries:

- Paul's I Corinthians 15 is the earliest account of the Resurrection.
- Resurrection is not resuscitation.
- Resurrection claims Jesus is the Christ, the Living One.
- Resurrection requires faith and cannot be proven by historical documentation or scientific fact.
- The two men in the tomb are examples of discipleship. Like the two men, the disciple is to proclaim the Resurrection.
- Just as for Peter, resurrection causes a type of amazement forcing us to wonder and ponder on its significance to our lives and the life of the community.

For Further Exploration

Jansen, John Frederick. *The Resurrection of Jesus Christ in New Testament Theology*. Philadelphia, Pa.: The Westminster Press, 1980.

Morris, Leon. *Luke: An Introduction and Commentary, Volume 3*, Tyndale New Testament Commentaries series. Grand Rapids, Mich.: Inter-Varsity Press; William B. Eerdmans Publishing Company, 1988.

Perkins, Pheme. *Resurrection: New Testament Witness and Contemporary Reflection*. Garden City, N.Y.: Doubleday & Company, Inc., 1984.

Journey 16
Post-Resurrectional Accounts

Journey 15 made claim to the fact that you cannot prove the Resurrection, you have to believe in it. One of the strongest demonstrations of belief is in witnessing. When we studied Paul's account of the Resurrection (I Corinthians 15), we noticed two parts: the core belief and the list of people who are believers. Paul states that Jesus died, was buried and rose. For Paul, the Resurrection occurred because Christ was *seen* by the Church community as represented in his listing of witnesses from Cephas (Peter) to himself, Paul. Throughout the history of Christianity, the proof of the Resurrection has been in the thousands of men and women who give witness to the fact that Jesus has risen from the dead.

Discovering

The story of the road to Emmaus is often considered the favorite narrative of many readers of Luke's Gospel. It is my favorite story because it is the culmination of many of the themes presented in his Gospel. In our study of this story, we will center on some of these themes.

Read Luke 24:13-35.

Throughout the rest of this Journey, I will ask you to paraphrase the sequence of events in this passage according to groups of verses and, then, for each event, write a statement that connects that event with a Lucan theme.

Paraphrase the events in Luke 24:13-16. Then write your statement that connects each event to a Lucan theme.

Lucan themes: There are two disciples, and they are moving away from Jerusalem. The specification that it was "two of them" recalls the Lucan theme of discipleship, of Christ sending them out in pairs (Luke 10:1).

The movement *away* from Jerusalem is significant. Jerusalem becomes symbolic of the journey with God. Where will we see God? We will see God in Jerusalem. Jesus' journey with God brings him to Jerusalem. Our journey with God will bring us to the *symbolic* Jerusalem, the place of faith. The action of the two people moving away from Jerusalem suggests a movement away from faith, not to faith and understanding.

The following sequence of events records their first meeting with Jesus. They are discussing all that had happened when Jesus approached them and started walking with them. However, they did not recognize him.

Although the account does not give the details of their discussion, we assume it was not a faith conversation because they are moving away from Jerusalem and they do not recognize Jesus. The major clue to their predicament is their inability to *see* Jesus. This is not a physical blindness, but a spiritual blindness in not seeing Jesus as the Lord. Their affliction is comparable to others within the Gospel who could not recognize Jesus as Lord.

Discovering

Paraphrase the sequence of events for Luke 24:17-31. Then write your statement that connects each event to a Lucan theme.

Exploring

The beginning of the story may be paraphrased in the following manner. Two people were going to Emmaus, which is seven miles away from Jerusalem. They were doing this on the same day that the women claimed Jesus' body was not in the tomb.

Two ideas within the first verse are connected with

Exploring

This section contains the body of the narrative. The story continues with a dialogue between Jesus and the two people (scholars differ on whether the two people were two men or a man and a woman, perhaps even husband and wife).

The dialogue begins with Jesus asking about their discussion and their questioning him if he is the only person in Jerusalem not to know of the past events (Luke 24:17-18).

In the discussion of the Passion, Jesus is accused of being prophet, king, Messiah. Although the accusation was correct, the accusers did not realize this. Likewise, these two people's reply to Jesus' question is equally ridiculous. Of all the people in Jerusalem the past few days, Jesus is the one who really did know what was going on!

The dialogue continues with the two providing an overview of Jesus' life. They mention that Jesus is a prophet, how he was crucified and their hope of his freeing Israel. They continue with the astonishing news that he was not in the tomb and how angels declared that Jesus was alive (Luke 24:19-24).

Jesus responds to their overview of his life by giving them a complete history that interprets every passage of Scripture (Luke 24:25-27).

The two people's overview of Jesus' life is incomplete when compared to Jesus' relating a complete history. They, like many others we met in the Gospel, have an incomplete picture of Jesus. Their references to Jesus are similar to those made of Moses who was a prophet powerful in word and deed and the liberator of Israel. However, even though they compare Jesus with Moses, their account does not appear as good news. Remember they are moving away from Jerusalem or moving away from faith. Jesus, in his account, demonstrates that he is greater than Moses, and it is only Jesus who fulfills *all* of the prophecies of the Old Testament.

The following sequence deals with their asking Jesus to remain with them and share a meal. At the meal, their eyes are opened (24:28-31).

The meal theme has been referred to numerous times in our journey with God through Jesus. At first, we may assume this to be a sacramental eucharistic meal and miss the point. The meal may be a eucharistic one since it is based on the theme of hospitality. But the point is Jesus was a stranger to them until they invited him to the meal. Once they invite an outsider to become an insider, they can see.

Discovering

Paraphrase the sequence of events and their connection to Lucan themes in Luke 24:32-35.

Exploring

On recognizing the stranger as Jesus, the Risen Lord, the two return to Jerusalem where they meet the Eleven. The entire group is aware that the Lord has risen. This is good news. When you realize that Jesus has conquered sin and death through the Resurrection, you run and share that news with all.

Discovering

Again, we need to reflect on the idea that resurrection is a matter of faith witnessed by believers. It cannot be proven by historical data or scientific fact.

With this idea of resurrection in mind, read the conclusion to Luke's Gospel. Read with biblical eyes. Read this conclusion aloud so that you may hear it with biblical ears.

Read Luke 24:36-51.

Write the insights you gained from reading with biblical eyes and listening with biblical ears.

Exploring

This final scene contains two parts: the appearance of Jesus to the disciples and the Ascension into heaven. In the appearance Jesus is not a vision or a ghost. He is real as demonstrated by the *real* act of showing wounds and eating a meal. The disciples are witnesses of this *real* Jesus, who is the Messiah (Luke 24:48). Witnesses do not remain in a protected area like this gathering place. Rather they begin where they are (Jerusalem) and spread the Good News to all the nations.

Obviously this message is not only for the gathered assembly of two thousand years ago. We are to be witnesses to the Resurrection and spread the Good News where we live and work. With the entire community proclaiming the Good News, the word of Jesus as the Christ will be shared with all nations, thus revealing that Christ's salvation is meant for all.

The Ascension of Jesus is not that he left them alone. If that was the case, then why are they "filled with joy" (Luke 24:52)? Jesus ascends to the Father which is the heavenly Jerusalem, another reference that the journey with God through Jesus leads to Jerusalem. The disciples return to Jerusalem to the Temple where they speak the praises of God.

This speaking the praises of God is the same as the recurring theme of prayer. Luke has taught us that prayer brings about the Spirit. Look at Luke 24:49, where Jesus instructs his disciples to "remain here in the city until you are clothed with power from on high." In one sense we conclude where we began: Prayer leads to the coming of the Spirit and the start of the mission. As disciples of Christ, we pray for the power of the Spirit to continue the mission of the Church.

Looking Back

On Journey 16 you made the following discoveries:

• The story of the disciples on the road to Emmaus is the culmination of many of the themes presented in Luke's Gospel.
• The movement away from Jerusalem signifies a movement away from faith.
• The recognition of Jesus as Lord allows us also to recognize Jesus in the stranger.
• The appearance of Jesus to the Eleven is proof that he has truly risen.
• The Ascension of Jesus to the Father is an ascension to the heavenly Jerusalem.
• The disciple is one who prays and receives the Spirit in order to continue the mission of the Church.

For Further Exploration

Fitzmyer, Joseph. *The Gospel According to Luke (X-XXIV)*, Anchor Bible Series. Garden City, N.Y.: Doubleday & Company, Inc., 1985.

LaVerdiere, Eugene. "Why Do You Seek the Living One Among the Dead?" *The Gospel of Luke*, Audiocassettes. Austin, Texas: Texas Catholic Conference Scripture Seminar, 1985.

Annotated Bibliography

Alday, Carrillo Salvador. *Power From On High: The Holy Spirit In The Gospels and Acts*. Ann Arbor, Mich.: Servant Books, 1978.

Alday presents an overview of the references to the Spirit in all of the Gospels plus the Book of Acts. His comments on the Spirit in the infancy story of Luke are helpful for understanding the connection between prayer and the Spirit. He traces Jesus' teaching on the Spirit while also supplying Old Testament roots to that teaching.

Anonymous. *The Cloud of Unknowing*. Middlesex, England: Penguin Books Ltd., 1961.

Written around the fourteenth century, this spiritual text is considered a masterpiece by many contemporary spiritual leaders. Its simple, but profound message is that God is not sought by the intellect but by love. It is in this love of God that the individual can overcome all obstacles set before one's life.

Apicella, Raymond. *Journeys Into Mark: 16 Lessons of Exploration and Discovery*. Cincinnati, Ohio: St. Anthony Messenger Press, 1990.

A companion piece to this manual on Luke, this book captures Mark's timely message and vital vision of the Christian life and teaches us how to live our Christian faith in these uncertain and troubled times.

Boadt, Lawrence. *Reading the Old Testament: An Introduction*. Mahwah, N.J.: Paulist Press, 1984.

Boadt provides as a textbook for beginning students of the Old Testament this comprehensive overview, which is clear and carefully organized. Pertinent to our study are his chapters on the Exodus/Sinai event. Students lacking a background in the Old Testament will find this book helpful. With a solid foundation in the Old Testament, the student will gain a greater appreciation for the New Testament.

Brown, Raymond E. *The Birth of the Messiah*. Garden City, N.Y.: Doubleday & Company, Inc., 1977.

For this complete commentary on the infancy narratives in Matthew and Luke, Raymond Brown researched numerous studies on every aspect of the birth stories of Jesus. Along with language and exegetical background, he supplies his comments on the material. This work is considered the most comprehensive work on the birth stories.

Brown, Raymond E., Joseph Fitzmyer, Roland Murphy, eds. *The New Jerome Biblical Commentary*, rev. ed. Englewood Cliffs, N.J.: Prentice Hall, 1990.

A major resource for biblical study, this commentary has been updated from the original 1969 edition to include the recent biblical understandings of the past twenty years. Robert Karris's comments on Luke are extremely helpful. The editors of this text are considered among the outstanding Catholic biblical scholars of our time.

Brown, Raymond E., et al, eds. *Mary in the New Testament*. Philadelphia, Pa.: Fortress Press, 1978.

This text on Mary is the result of a combined effort by the Lutheran World Federation and the National Conference of Catholic Bishops. Its purpose is to present the role of Mary from a biblical perspective rather than a doctrinal one. The Protestant and Catholic scholars who contribute to this work arrive at an image of Mary thought to be held by early Christians.

Conzelmann, Hans. *The Theology of St. Luke*. New York, N.Y.: Harper & Row Publishers, Inc., 1960.

Conzelmann's text is considered the classical work on Luke. Other commentators often begin their study with this work. His research is extremely helpful in understanding Luke's use of geography and his concept of God's redemptive acts.

Fitzmyer, Joseph A. *Luke the Theologian: Aspects of His Teaching*. Mahwah, N.J.: Paulist Press, 1989.

In this excellent text on Luke's major theological themes, Fitzmyer supports the idea that Luke is presenting various themes to the Christian community. He discusses eight of these themes. His comments on Satan and his work on discipleship are especially helpful.

—.*The Gospel According to Luke (I-IX)*, Anchor Bible Series. Garden City, N.Y.: Doubleday & Company, Inc., 1985.

Each detail of Luke's writing undergoes a critical review by Fitzmyer. His understanding of biblical Greek and ability to do exegesis makes this text an excellent companion when reading Luke's Gospel.

—.*The Gospel According to Luke (X-XXIV)*, Anchor Bible Series. Garden City, N.Y.: Doubleday & Company, Inc., 1985.

This second volume of Fitzmyer's commentary reviews Chapters 10-24 of Luke's Gospel. Fitzmyer's comments on the Passion, Resurrection and Ascension were the foundation for some ideas presented in the Journeys.

Flanagan, Neil. *Mark, Matthew, and Luke: A Guide to the Gospel Parallels*. Collegeville, Minn.: The Liturgical Press, 1978.

In this guide to Burton Throckmorton's text, *Gospel Parallels*, Flanagan shares classroom notes from his teaching courses. His section on Luke's Gospel provides an excellent background to the themes in Luke, the parallel writing structure of both the Gospel and the Book of Acts, as well as comments on the time, place and author of this Gospel.

Guinan, Michael. *Gospel Poverty: Witness to the Risen Christ*. Ramsey, N.J.: Paulist Press, 1981.

Guinan outlines the understanding of poverty in both the Old and New Testaments. He holds that the biblical word, *anawim*, for poverty suggests something more than economics. For Guinan, he sees *anawim* as a dependence or weakness. This text provides excellent background for understanding the beatitude: "Blest are the poor...."

Hall, T. William, Richard Pilgrim, Ronald Cavanagh. *Religion: An Introduction*. San Francisco, Calif.: Harper & Row Publishers, 1985.

The three authors are professors at Syracuse University and wrote this text for their undergraduate courses on religion. The text covers the broad nature of religion. It concentrates on a definition of religion as well as a variety of religious expressions, such as sacred stories, ritual, myth, and morality.

Jansen, John Frederick. *The Resurrection of Jesus Christ in New Testament Theology*. Philadelphia, Pa.: The Westminster Press, 1980.

Jansen does not concentrate on one Gospel account of the Resurrection. Rather, he describes the significance of the Resurrection in terms of the *whole* New Testament. He continues to ask the question, "What does the Resurrection mean?" as a way of discovering its significance for the present age. For Jansen, the Resurrection is the important event of our past, present and future.

Karris, Robert. *Invitation to Luke: A Commentary on the Gospel of Luke With Complete Text From The Jerusalem Bible*. Garden City, N.Y.: Image Books, 1977.

In his commentary on Luke's Gospel Karris provides excellent information on the Church and world from which Luke writes. Karris supplies short essays on missionary work, persecution and community problems.

——. *Luke: Artist and Theologian*. Mahwah, N.J.: Paulist Press, 1985.

Robert Karris provides deeper insights into an understanding of Luke than he does in his other commentaries. He discusses various Lucan themes while placing significant emphasis on the justice and meal themes. Students interested in further information on these two topics would do well to read this text.

——. *What Are They Saying About Luke and Acts?* Mahwah, N.J.: Paulist Press, 1979.

Karris traces themes found in both Luke's Gospel and the Book of Acts. This book is a good resource for those wishing to further study the parallel between Luke's Gospel and Acts.

LaVerdiere, Eugene. *The Gospel of Luke*, Audiocassettes. Austin, Texas: Texas Catholic Conference Scripture Seminar, 1985.

These audiocassettes were produced from a four-day seminar on Luke's Gospel. LaVerdiere goes beyond many points published in his commentary by Glazier (see entry below). His explanation of neighbor and meal, and techniques for studying Luke are highlighted in this manual.

——. *Luke*. New Testament Message, Vol. 5. Wilmington, Del.: Michael Glazier, Inc., 1983.

This volume is part of an entire commentary on the New Testament. LaVerdiere supplies a portion of the New Testament account and then a commentary on the Scripture presented. The complete set would be an excellent supplementary guide for people desiring more information on any passage of Luke's Gospel.

——. *When We Pray: Meditation on the Lord's Prayer*. Notre Dame, Ind.: Ave Maria Press, 1983.

This is LaVerdiere's marvelous work on the Our Father and the foundation for the comments in Journey 9. LaVerdiere suggests the Lord's Prayer is a prayer to the Spirit by a disciple.

Merton, Thomas. *Our Father: Perfect Prayer*, Audiocassette. Kansas City, Mo.: Credence Cassettes, 1989.

Given as a lecture to novices from the Abbey of Our Lady, Gethsemani, Merton traces the power of the prayer from its scriptural roots through the early Church. When listening to Merton, you can make a connection to LaVerdiere's thought that this prayer is a prayer to the Spirit. Merton refers to the Lord's Prayer as a "prayer of fire."

Morris, Leon. *Luke: An Introduction and Commentary, Vol. 3*, Tyndale New Testament Commentaries series. Grand Rapids, Mich.: Inter-Varsity Press; William B. Eerdmans Publishing Company, 1988.

As a commentary, this text provides excellent background to understanding the time, place and dating of Luke's Gospel. Similar to other commentaries, it supplies information on the various themes presented within the Gospel.

Pennington, Basil. *Daily We Touch Him: Practical Religious Experience*. Garden City, N.Y.: Doubleday and Company, 1977.

Basil Pennington is a Trappist monk at St. Joseph's Abbey, Spencer, Massachusetts. He has traveled and lectured extensively on the spiritual life. This text provides the basic framework for incorporating concepts acquired from *The Cloud of Unknowing* into one's daily routine. Pennington especially emphasizes that the contemporary person can find spiritual value by developing a rule of life, practicing centering prayer and obtaining a spiritual director.

Perkins, Pheme. *Love Commands in the New Testament*. Ramsey, N.Y.: Paulist Press, 1982.

Perkins presents an understanding of what she refers to as the cultural setting of New Testament ethics. She provides excellent background to the notion of loving your enemy (Luke 6). Two of her chapters, Chapter 4 and Chapter 5, comment on the Prodigal Son and Good Samaritan stories from Luke's Gospel.

——. *Reading the New Testament*, 2nd ed. Mahwah, N.J.: Paulist Press, 1988.

Perkins' textbook is an excellent introduction for beginning students of the New Testament. She provides a clear and comprehensive background for understanding how the Scriptures came to be. Her comments on Paul, as well as her chapter on Luke, are helpful.

——. *Resurrection: New Testament Witness and Contemporary Reflection*. Garden City, N.Y.: Doubleday & Company, Inc., 1984.

Perkins' work on the Resurrection is considered one of the classical presentations on the subject. She traces resurrection from its Old Testament roots to its preaching by the early Church. Perkins provides additional information to the meal theme and its implications for the road to Emmaus story.

Rohr, Richard. *Working for Justice*, Video program. Miami, Fla.: St. Thomas University, 1990.

Rohr, a frequent visitor to St. Thomas University, speaks to undergraduate students on the topic of peace and justice. The focus of his presentation is that peace and justice are at the heart of where we discover truth. This discovery of truth is not merely a matter of the head but rather an integration of all that makes up humankind in order to bring about the true message of God. In order to discover this truth of God, Rohr suggests some interesting views on particular Gospel passages.

Schottroff, Luise, and Wolfgang Stegemann. *Jesus and the Hope of the Poor*. Maryknoll, N.Y.: Orbis Books, 1986.

These authors place the teachings and actions of Jesus within the Jewish community. They claim that Jesus is a symbol of hope for the oppressed and poor of his time. One of this text's major themes is that Jesus is the savior for sinners and the despised.

Schweizer, Eduard. *The Good News According to Luke*. Atlanta: John Knox Press, 1984.

Schweizer prepares his commentary with an emphasis that Luke is teaching us about God. In a description of the text, Schweizer claims that the term *God* is used 122 times in the Gospel and 166 times in Acts, considerably more than in the other Gospels. His commentary, as do the others, gives clarification to the idea that we are on a journey to God through Christ.

The Works of Josephus, trans. William Whiston. Peabody, Mass.: Hendrickson Publishers, 1985.

Josephus was a Jewish historian during the first century. His work is excellent background material for understanding the times, politics and religious influences during the period of Christ and the early Church.

Throckmorton, Burton, ed. *Gospel Parallels: A Synopsis of the First Three Gospels*, rev. ed. Nashville, Tenn.: Thomas Nelson, Inc., 1979.

This text is helpful in viewing the Synoptic writers in parallel columns. By training the eye to read a Gospel passage while looking at the parallel to other writers, the reader quickly notices Q material, shared material or individual sources. This text is a marvelous tool for beginning students of Scripture.